Ⓑ 8.75

La Tristesse de Saint Louis

Also by Mike Zwerin

Close Enough For Jazz: An Autobiography

A Case for the Balkanization of Practically Everyone

The Silent Sound of Needles

MIKE ZWERIN

La Tristesse de Saint Louis: Jazz Under the Nazis

BEECH TREE BOOKS
WILLIAM MORROW
New York

Copyright © 1985 by Mike Zwerin

All rights reserved. No part of this book may be
reproduced or utilized in any form or by any
means, electronic or mechanical, including
photocopying, recording or by any information
storage and retrieval system, without permission in
writing from the Publisher. Inquiries should be
addressed to Permissions Department, Beech Tree
Books, William Morrow and Company, Inc., 105
Madison Ave., New York, N.Y. 10016.

Library of Congress Cataloging-in-Publication Data

Zwerin, Michael.
  La tristesse de Saint Louis.

  (Beech tree books)
  Reprint. Originally published: London; New
York:
Quartet books, 1985.
  Includes index.
  1. Jazz music—Germany—World War,
1939–1945.
I. Title.
ML3509.G47Z9   1987   785.42'094   86-16169
ISBN 0-688-06537-6

Printed in the United States of America

First U.S. Edition

1 2 3 4 5 6 7 8 9 10

BℓB

The word "book" is said to derive from *boka*, or beech.
The beech tree has been the patron tree of writers since ancient times and
represents the flowering of literature and knowledge.

For Anne Zwerin

Thanks to Dietrich Schulz-Koehn, Charles Delaunay, Otto Jung, Hans Bluthner, Carlo Bohlander, Paula Klein, Josef Balcerak, Emil Mangelsdorff, Albert Mangelsdorff, Svend Asmussen, Anna Kulicka, Heinz Baldauf, Louis Vola, Pawel Brodowski, Diz Disley, Frank Tenot, Wolfgang Muth, Joachim-Ernst Berendt, Jean Sablon, Joseph Reinhardt, Carlos de Radzitzky, Michael Haggerty, Helle Horup, Stephane Grappelli, Ib Skovgaard, Gerald Arnaud, Maurice Cullaz, Marc Albert, John Sparrow, Hans Kumpf, Mary Phillips, Hart Leroy Bibbs, Maurice Girodias, Major Emil Engels, Wieslaw Machan, Edmund Fetting, Adam Linkowski, Alexei Batashev, Keith Knox, Al Lirvat, Nicholas Dor, Dieter Zimmerle, John Schults, Josef Skvorecky, Micheline Day, Ole Matthiessen, Lance Tschannen, Erwin Goldman, Gene Lees, Phil Lees, Paul Breslin, Gilles Aaronson, Martine Halphen, Benjamin Zwerin and Kaypro.

Photographs of Ghetto Swingers and concentration camps courtesy of Wolfgang Muth *Jazz Forum* magazine; of Herb Flemming, Arne Halphers, Jack Hylton, Henry Hall, Ernst Van't Hoff, Jean Omer, Dietrich Schulz-Koehn, Otto Jung, Carlo Bohlander, Hughes Panassié, Edith Piaf and Django Reinhardt, Django and Stephane Grappelli, Charles Delaunay, Django and Pierre Fouad, Delaunay and Django courtesy of Otto Jung; of Louis Armstrong's letter, Armstrong in Berlin, Lester Young in Berlin courtesy of Hans Bluthner; of Carlo Bohlander, Charly Petri and Black Charlie, Frankfurt friends' band 1944 courtesy of Carlo Bohlander; other photographs and illustrations courtesy of Anna Kulicka, Charles Delaunay, Dietrich Schulz-Koehn and Jos Linssen.

Portions of this book have appeared in the *International Herald Tribune, Sphere* and *Jazz Hot* magazines.

Contents

From a poster from a Nazi exhibition concerned with decadent (*Entartete*) music

I have set before the reader not an analysed summary of my researches but an account of the search itself

A.J.A. Symons, *The Quest for Corvo*

Introduction

The time: roughly 1933 through to the present. Very roughly. It's a rough story.

The place: the Third Reich, occupied Europe, unoccupied Europe, Sad Afrika and present-day Warsaw and Paris.

The subject: I started out to write a sort of hipster history of World War II, to explore a neglected corner of history, but it overran me. Literally. I was flattened, squashed, blitzkrieged. Eventually the 'subject' was no longer the subject. It became subjective. It overran the original definitions of time and place. The subject includes what happened to me while writing this book because I was writing it.

The form: personal chronology, what happened to me next.

Certain stories were almost the same from country to country, with different names and dates. The most interesting and evocative version was used.

Accuracy came first, but when there was a choice between poetry and journalism, I picked poetry. No attempt has been made to be encyclopaedic. You will not find out who played third trumpet with Ernst Van't Hoff's band in Berlin in 1941. Or maybe you will.

The facts: specified names, dates and places are factual, though after more than three years' work, it became difficult to separate imagination from fact. Imagination itself became one more fact. Imaginative facts are always presented as such. Some characters are composites, but this is always obvious from their names.

1
The Third Reich in 4/4 Time

Luftwaffe Oberleutnant Dietrich Schulz-Koehn walked along the railroad tracks near St Nazaire with three other officers. Four American officers came towards them down the line. Small-arms fire could be heard in the distance.

The winter of 1944 was cold. The men danced and blew on their hands. The day was grey, like an old print of a black-and-white war movie. They had minor roles. It was a sideshow. The main theatre had moved east to the Fatherland.

One hundred thousand German soldiers were cut off and worn out here on the Brittany coast. The Allies were prepared to starve them out, but civilians were starving too and the Red Cross arranged evacuation negotiations along these tracks, an hour a day for two weeks now. The opposing sides began to fraternize. They took photographs of each other, traded the prints.

Today, an Afro-American officer who had been admiring Schulz-Koehn's Rolleiflex asked: 'How much do you want for that camera?'

'It's not for sale.' The lanky, bespectacled German liked Americans, particularly Afro-Americans. He was more than pleasant about it, but he liked his camera too.

'How about three cartons of Luckies and four pairs of nylons?'

No, that was not enough, but as a matter of fact there was something. Why not? A few beats went by. The war was almost over anyway. Schulz-Koehn straightened up and adjusted his leather coat. It was worth a try: 'Do you have any Count Basie records?'

2
Snarls

When the German commander asked besieged Bastogne, Belgium, to surrender during the Battle of the Bulge, defending American General McAuliffe snarled: 'Nuts!'

'Nuts' is such an innocent, archaic euphemism. These days generals snarl 'Balls!' or worse. 'Nuts' comes out of Andy Hardy movies and Dick Tracy comic strips, from a time when it was clear who the good and bad guys were and good guys did not say 'Balls!' even when they snarled.

I was driving north from Paris to Bastogne, in the Ardennes, and then to the Ruhr to speak with elderly gentlemen who would never snarl, let alone say 'Balls!' They are good guys who were considered bad guys by good guys ('no such thing as a good German'), and monkeys by the beasts who ruled them.

The fastest route from Paris to the Ruhr is not through the Ardennes, but I wanted some snarls to put the monkeys in context; I could say hello to 'Blow' Black in Aachen after I spoke with the major; and I had an appointment in Liege first to meet Nicolas Dor.

One evening during the autumn of 1941, Nicolas Dor was listening to Lester Young records in a bar in Liege. It was owned by three sisters, who also ran the bordello upstairs. One of them came and whispered: 'Those two German officers over there want to talk to you.'

Dor did not want to talk to them. 'I don't speak German,' he said.

'They speak English,' she pleaded.

She was a friend. He was a regular. They did not want trouble.

The madam introduced him: 'This is the drummer I told you about.'

Dor was leading a combo modelled after John Kirby, his idol. They played benefits for Belgian prisoners of war – 'Every Tub' by Count Basie, '920 Special', pieces like that. Radio Brussels' programme from 7–9 a.m., which had an enormous audience of people getting ready to go to work, featured a jazz band. Jazz musicians played in clubs all night until curfew ended at six, then went to the radio station. And there were plenty of places to play for lunch. World War II was the golden age of Belgian jazz.

'We understand you have some Jimmie Lunceford records,' one of the Germans said, trying a bit too hard to be friendly. 'We'd like to listen to them sometimes. We're trumpet players.' They said they had worked with Jack Hylton, a famous English bandleader influenced by Paul Whiteman, before the war.

Though they might be brothers under the uniforms, the connotation was unmistakable. It was an order one way or another. And who could be sure they were what they said they were? Dor gave them his address reluctantly.

Three days later, he was dining with his parents when the doorbell rang. His mother went to the window and exclaimed: 'German officers!'

Dor peeked through the curtain. 'It's all right,' he reassured her, 'they're friends of mine.' He suspected that his mother suspected him of collaborating, until, over a cup of coffee, one of the officers said to her: 'If you have any trouble about your son being sent to Germany, call me.' Impressed labourers were leaving every day. He wrote down his phone number.

Dor and the Germans went to his room and listened to 'Americano nigger kike jungle music' for hours.

The quote is from Joseph Goebbels, who had banned jazz, along with foxtrots and the tango. Although repulsed by the 'terrible squawk' of jazz, he soon realized that swing between the harangues held listeners. The extent of the ban and the definition of the music had both been vague anyway. Nobody has ever really succeeded in defining jazz, which is one reason I love it so much.

Until just before the Battle of the Bulge, the Stan Branders big band played music by American Jewish and black composers over Radio Brussels without hiding the names. ' "Softly as in a Morning Sunrise" by Sigmund Romberg,' he'd announce. ' "J'ai du Rythme" by George Gershwin'; ' "Duke's Idea" by Charlie Barnet'. If this music was illegal, nobody seemed to be enforcing.

So it was not clear whether Dor and the Germans were breaking a law. He looked carefully up and down the street before showing them out.

Two months later he received the order to report for a physical examination. He called the German, who came, took notes, and said: 'Go, but tell them you already received the same order.'

'This is the second time I've had to come here with a piece of paper like this,' Dor told the clerk, who signalled to his supervising officer. They scratched their heads checking the file. The clerk pulled out a document: 'You never received a copy of this?'

He tried to remain calm. It was an official exemption, slipped into the file by a German trumpet player, citing a non-existent tubercular condition. 'No,' he said, 'never.'

Annoyed by a breakdown in Aryan efficiency, the supervisor stamped it and Dor spent the rest of the war playing John Kirby tunes.

Forty years later, a producer for Belgian French-language TV, he smiled in the bright Broadcasting House dining-room and said: 'So you see? Jazz saved my life.'

It was a cruel day in the Ardennes. Fields were flooded, rivers swollen. Gusts of wind shook the trees, the sky was a volatile, ominous series of grey-and-black swirls. Occasional spots of snow on the fields became a blanket and I ran into ice and a blizzard as the road rose.

The crawling line of traffic stopped dead on a steep hill. I pulled the handbrake another notch and switched the windshield wiper to fast. Up ahead the police were dealing with a snowbound semi-trailer blocking the road. I looked at my watch. The major was waiting. Nuts!

In the midst of World War II, Dietrich Schulz-Koehn had published an illegal jazz newsletter with articles in praise of 'Americano nigger kike jungle music' and flattering portraits of those who played it.

Schulz-Koehn's illegal newsletter reprinted (in English) a piece titled 'Real Musician' by Norman Sullivan from a 1938 *Saturday*

Evening Post, exactly the sort of 'decadence' the Germans were being told that it was honourable to die fighting to exterminate. He had sent me a cassette of himself reading it; I slipped it into the machine:

Q: Are you a musician, Mr Snipeworthy?
A: Yes, I'm a gate with a . . .
Q: A gate?
A: Yeah. I can swing way out wide. I'm a gate with a solid send of jive.
Q: A solid send of what?
A: Jive. The stuff that's mellow. It sends you right out of this world if you've got an alligator ear.
Q: Not so fast, Mr Snipeworthy. I don't understand.
A: An alligator ear is what hep-cats have got. It means you know good music, you're not an icky.
Q: And why were you speeding on Main Street?
A: I was going after a dotmaker to keep a date to make a platter.
Q: Stop! Confine yourself to English. What is a dotmaker?
A: A guy who writes musical arrangements. We was hurryin' to make a platter – I mean to cut the wax – that is, make a record. Well, just then the solid-beat man . . .
Q: Hold on! The solid-beat man?
A: The drummer. He looked at his watch and saw we was late. We'd been to a little E-flat meetin' . . .
Q: An E-flat meetin'. What's that?
A: Just a little unimportant engagement, your honour. Where the band can't ride because it's mostly paper-men.
Q: What are they?
A: Guys who just play the notes. Some of 'em can play maybe an honest trumpet, but not a go trumpet, see? Not real dixieland.
Q: You are a member of a good band?
A: Oh sure, we can really send. We really get ridin' and lick our whiskers. We go right into it and jubit.
Q: Jubit?
A: Yeah, kick it, break it down. We're murderistic. We beat you right down to your socks, send you swing-happy. Your honour, we just dream it up.
Q: Well, I'm letting you go, but don't do any more speeding in

this town. I realize you probably couldn't read our road signs, written in English. Case dismissed.

'It was cockeyed,' Schulz-Koehn had told me, 'if we had been caught it could have meant big trouble. But we were young and foolish, and we so much loved the music.'

Frozen in traffic, I looked at the snow-laden thick forest on both sides of the road. It reminded me of a passage from Charles B. Macdonald's history of the Battle of the Bulge, which had been fought around here:

Once magnificent trees were now twisted, gashed, broken . . . some trees stood like gaunt, outsized toothpicks. Great jagged chunks of concrete and twisted reinforcing rods that together had been a pillbox. The mutilated carcass of a truck that had hit a mine. Everywhere discarded soldier equipment – gas masks, empty rations containers, helmets, rifles, here a field jacket with a sleeve rent, there a muddy overcoat with an ugly clotted dark stain on it. One man kicked a bloody shoe from his path, then shuddered that the shoe still had a foot in it . . . Here and there bodies of the dead lay about in grotesque positions, weather-soaked, bloated, the stench from them cloying . . .

When the semi cleared, I slid into Bastogne for an appointment with Major Emil Engels of the Belgian army. There was no mistaking him. He had told me laughing over the phone that he would be 'dressed for battle'. He slapped the snow from his beret and brushed off his fatigues: 'This will give you a pretty good idea of the weather then. Only it was colder: ten below, centigrade.'

He told me about the Germans and what motivated them, their rules and personality traits and explained why they were the ultimate losers. He named divisions by number and complement, evaluated morale, specified commanding officers – a passionate, scholarly dissertation.

Some time previously, a German scholar had answered my request for information pertaining to jazz under the Nazis by writing: 'I am quite surprised by your letter. There are dozens of people still alive who have suffered under the Nazis for their love for jazz; there are hundreds of articles written about this subject, thousands of documents – all in German – and here comes Mike Zwerin who has never much cared about this subject and who isn't able to read the documents because he doesn't speak German and wants to write a book about it. I expect this to become another model of careless journalism. I am writing about this subject since more than thirty years; many other people have done the same ... Considering the subject is new to you and you are new to this subject I guess you have to live two or three years in Germany in order to meet all the people and interview them and study all the articles and books.'

My subject is European not German; I am fluent in French; translators are for hire. I wrote a book about European national minorities without speaking Basque, Welsh or Lappish; and one about junkies although I'm no junky. Outsiders can have a broader perspective – and learning along with the reader makes good drama. And I cared so much I was about to lose twelve kilos and almost ruin my life. So much for careless journalism.

Germans make terrific heavies. People of other European nationalities frequently speak of the Third Reich with a certain nostalgia, as though grateful to have been able to count on such indisputable devils. Watching an old war movie on TV the other night, I realized, about twenty minutes into it, that we had not seen a German soldier yet and that I missed them. When the Wehrmacht finally arrived, I shocked my wife France by cheering. France lost aunts and uncles in the camps and as far as she's concerned, there never was and will never be a good German. But I was happy to see them. We need our devils.

On 15 December 1944, the eve of what was to be the final blitzkrieg, Field-Marshal Gerd von Rundstedt sent a message to his twenty camouflaged divisions massed east of the Ardennes: 'Tomorrow we gamble everything.' The Americans across the lines were also looking forward to the sixteenth; Marlene Dietrich was scheduled to perform for the 99th infantry.

The Allies had been advancing through Belgium towards the German border since September; Hitler's personal last-ditch battle plan called for a race back via Bastogne to capture the port of Antwerp.

Clues were ignored: German hospital trains marshalling on the banks of the Rhine, flatcars shuttling tanks towards the Ardennes, heavy road traffic at night, two Panzer divisions suddenly disappearing from intelligence maps, captured German prisoners displaying unusually high morale for 'defeated' soldiers.

When one American intelligence officer predicted a major German offensive in the Ardennes, it was diagnosed as battle fatigue and he was in Paris on leave when the German 'Bulge' began pushing towards the Meuse river. It would be the biggest battle of the war in Western Europe, a fierce battle on rough mountain terrain in the middle of a hard winter. The Germans gambled everything and lost.

The major recounted the siege of Bastogne like a western. In westerns, pioneers put their wagons in a circle, they shoot at the Indians and wait for the cavalry to rescue them, which of course it always does, just in time. Always from the south. And who's leading them? John Wayne. The cavalry broke into Bastogne just in time from the south led by General Patton – John Wayne. The major clapped his hands with the perfection of it.

We were parked in Houffalize, a wide spot in the road. These small junctions circling Bastogne became strategic during the siege. Soldiers fought all day to capture a farmhouse just for a warm place to sleep. Through the flapping wipers, we watched three small children climb over a German tank on the corner, one of many such monuments; children do not forget World War II around here.

'That tank belonged to the 116th Panzer division.' The major pointed: 'See the number 401 painted on the turret? To the right is a small insignia with a greyhound dog over a wavy line with what looks like three blades of grass. Only two weeks ago I discovered the meaning of the insignia. The 116th fought in Russia. This particular tank fought in Stalingrad and Bastogne. The division found a greyhound in Russia, adopted it as a mascot and called it Sacha. I've seen photos of the 116th in Normandy in 1944 – there are greyhounds with them. The wavy line and the grass probably represent the Russian steppes. They may seem unimportant to other people, but I love details like that.'

People are frequently nostalgic for war because it was the only excitement in their lives. And because they did not have to search for 'meaning'. Later they worked, had families, retired. Peace, the absence of strife, is boring. Elderly European jazz musicians of many nationalities sighed with pleasure remembering World War

II – their youth, all the gigs they could handle, no American competition, everybody loved jazz. 'It was the Golden Age,' I kept hearing; and, 'Those were such wonderful days. Please don't misunderstand, but . . .'

The Battle of the Bulge was the most exciting thing to happen in Bastogne in at least a century. The battle museum is a tourist attraction and the chamber of commerce sells memorial booklets. A municipal sign on Place McAuliffe, the town centre, proclaims the place: 'Nuts City'.

In October 1974, Major William Desobry, by then a general, came to Bastogne on a pilgrimage at the same time as the German ex-general Hasso von Manteuffel. Thirty years earlier, they had opposed each other in a bloody engagement around the crossroads of Noville.

'There is something I've been wanting to ask you,' Desobry said. 'At one point you just stopped your tanks. You had destroyed us. If you had kept going you could have been in Bastogne in an hour. Why didn't you do it?'

'That's American reasoning, you see,' the German answered. 'In your army you left field commanders certain initiative. But a German general had to go to Berlin if he wanted even minor modifications in the plan of battle.'

When, later, I told a friend, Carlton Laughs, the von Manteuffel story over the phone, he said: 'That's the Germans all right.'

Laughs had just arrived in Paris after a week in Stuttgart where he produced a breakdance and rap spectacular: 'I'll give you another example. The show was televised by German TV. One camera was in our way and we asked the operator to move a couple of inches. Inches. Would you believe that he had to call over the director and the producer so they could approve it first? "Just following orders," he said.'

The story doesn't hold. A cameraman anywhere might have done the same thing. It's always easy to find objective proof of preconceived prejudice. I admit to mixed feelings about Germany. I suppose I have a weak spot for German comfort. Oiled, upholstered, over-designed, muted, the country glides along nicely on certain levels. The phones work, heating systems are adequate, the cities are orderly and quiet and there's a special soothing solidity to German residential suburbs. Trouble is, everyone over sixty should be bugged. You never know. There is something soiled about a place where youths can't be sure about their grandparents. And I suppose you could call it 'fat' rather than 'solid'. They are proud of their fat. Fat is essential to German comfort. They snarl when it's threatened.

I held the receiver away from my ear as Laughs warmed up to the subject: 'The promoter implied that business would have been better if our artists had been white. Imagine, white rappers! The Germans are all racist. That's hardly news, but you hear a lot of nice things about young Germans, and frankly I don't see it. You get the feeling that if the hot water doesn't come on this morning the Nazis could be back tomorrow afternoon. They're so easily manipulated. It's in the culture. Everybody's a cop. I was parking my car illegally and a woman picked up an SOS phone on the spot to fink to the precinct.

'Listen, my wife and I took a walk one afternoon. We were staying in a hotel in the suburbs and there was this large, beautiful park nearby. You know, little walk in the park. We heard a lot of commotion and when we got closer there were three guys wearing thick gloves and special padded sleeves and trousers training German attack dogs. The dogs were snarling. So were the guys.'

I took leave of the major around six, drove to Aachen, checked into a hotel, drew a hot bath, opened my reading file and pulled out a photocopy of 'Swing and Nigger Music Must Disappear' by 'Buschmann' from the 6 November 1938 edition of a Stettin newspaper:

Disgusting things are going on, disguised as 'entertainment'. We have no sympathy for fools who want to transplant jungle music to Germany. In Stettin, like other cities, one can see people dancing as though they suffer from stomach pains. They call it 'swing'. This is no joke. I am overcome with anger.

These people are mentally retarded. Only niggers in some jungle would stomp like that. Germans have no nigger in them. The pandemonium of swing fever must be stopped.

We are not prudes, on the contrary. Everybody should work to do their part in building a greater Reich, but after this work they have the right to enjoy themselves. People who cannot enjoy themselves cannot work properly either. We are not afraid to say 'yes' to life.

Everyone should be able to enjoy the entertainment they prefer. One goes to the opera in the evening, another to the cinema, a third to the theatre. Maybe a boy wants to go out and dance with his girlfriend. Well and good. But there are limits.

Impresarios who present swing dancing should be put out of business. Swing orchestras that play hot, scream on their instruments, stand up to solo and other cheap devices are going to disappear. Nigger music must disappear.

Then I went to hear Blow Black. Except for a few cats on stools, the club was empty around ten when Blow Black finally arrived. The music should have started hours ago. The customers had all gone home. The gentle snow had turned to pounding rain, though there were still intense flurries inside Blow's nose. He went directly to the men's room mumbling something about 'an act of God on the autobahn'.

Blow had been on staff with a Düsseldorf radio and TV house orchestra with paid vacations, medical insurance and a retirement plan since we had both arrived in Europe fifteen years ago. He works with his own band a couple of nights a week. Though he reminds himself that back home in Cleveland he'd be just one more scuffling brother, the 'German miracle' notwithstanding, he was coming unglued.

He decided to refuse to speak German to the orchestra leader, who complained to the union about it, and about his dreadlocks. 'I'll cut his neck,' Blow fumed to the mediators, 'before I cut my hair.'

I've seen it often. 'The Claw'. Eventually, it clutches inside the heads of all hard-core cocaine users and you can almost see it through the scalp. I don't understand why people in general and creative people in particular pay so much money to put themselves in such a state. It is the perfect state of mind for robbing a bank. When the owner, who seemed civilized and on strong moral and legal ground, refused to pay, Blow screamed 'Fucking Nazi!' He landed a right cross on the owner's chin before throwing his trumpet through a plate-glass window.

'Kraut coke!' Blow snarled with a straight face. 'Turns you into a fucking stormtrooper. But if they think they can make a good German out of me they're nuts.'

Was ist Niggerjazz?

Musik, die im Rundfunk verboten ist

Bekanntlich hat Reichssendeleiter Habamovsky anläßlich der letzten Intendanten-Tagung in München den Niggerjazz im Rundfunk endgültig verboten. Da vielfach über den Begriff des „Niggerjazzes" noch Unklarheit zu bestehen scheint, dürften die nachstehenden grundsätzlichen Ausführungen in der „Preußischen Zeitung" besonders interessieren.

Was den undeutschen Jazz von zeitgemäßer deutscher Tanzmusik unterscheidet, sind die gleichen Merkmale, die auf dem ganzen Gebiete der Musik sich als zersetzend eingenistet haben. Es entspricht unserer rassischen Bedingtheit, daß wir eine Musik dann als schön und angenehm empfinden, wenn sie erstens eine Melodie enthält, zweitens harmonisch klingt und drittens klar und sauber instrumentiert ist. Mit dieser Feststellung scheiden also für unser deutsches Empfinden aus:

1. Stücke ohne Melodienführung, bei denen nur ein kurzes armseliges Schlagerthema lediglich rhythmisch weitergeführt und in phantasielosen Variationen zu Tode gehetzt wird, bis sich diese Musik am Schluß — übrigens durchaus logischerweise (!) — in ein Fragezeichen auflöst.

2. Stücke, die statt den Hörer in harmonischem Zusammenklang zu erfreuen, ihn in atonalen Akkorden zerquälen, eine Musik, die entweder einer krankhaften Seelenverfassung entspringt, oder aber, wie es meistens der Fall ist, nur mit dem Verstande ergrübelt ist, um krampfhaft als Sensation aufzufallen. Sie stammt nie aus dem Herzen einer musikalischen Seele und kann deshalb nie den Weg zum Herzen des Hörers finden, sondern günstigstenfalls von volksfremden blasierten Snobs als „interessant empfunden werden.

3. Alle Stücke, die in ihrer Instrumentierung eine klare Tonbildung vermissen lassen, bei denen alle oder einzelne Instrumente lediglich Geräusche machen, sei es nun, ob sie an quälende Kindertrompeten erinnern, wie insbesondere die gestopfte Jazztrompete, oder sei es das reichliche Handwerkszeug des Schlagzeugers, soweit es nicht harmonisch abgestimmt und diskret in die Begleitung eingefügt ist. Kennzeichnend für den Jazz ist weiter das starke Hervortreten des Saxophons, das nicht als Orchesterstimme behandelt wird, um mit den anderen Instrumenten zusammen einen farbigen Wohlklang zu ergeben, sondern aufdringlich allein die Melodie führt, während alle anderen Instrumente lediglich den Rhythmus betonen und hetzen. Eine solche Orchestrierung gibt der Tanzweise ein fratzenhaftes Gesicht. Sie sucht sich durch den Rhythmus einzuhämmern und systematisch jedes gesunde Gefühl für Wohllaut abzustumpfen.

Mit diesen Merkmalen, die keineswegs erschöpfend sind, sondern nur das Wesentliche hervorheben sollen, ist bei weitem der größte Teil der unser Ohr beleidigenden Jazzmusik gekennzeichnet und aus der Betrachtung ausgeschieden. Was noch übrig bleibt an synkopischer zeitgenössischer Tanzmusik wird am sichersten in seinem Gesamteindruck durch ein instinktsicheres Gefühl als deutsch oder undeutsch empfunden bzw. abgelehnt werden können. Hierbei wird das Entscheidende sein, ob wir es als frisch, lebhaft mit heiterem Naturell empfinden, oder als sinnlich schwül und gequält. Dies gilt nicht nur für moderne Tanzweisen im synkopischen Rhythmus. Hierbei sei besonders auch an die übersüßlich schmachtenden Tonfilmschlager meist amerikanischen Ursprungs erinnert. Allerdings muß hier gesagt werden, daß unser Gefühl infolge jahrelanger Gewöhnung an die Jazzmusik uns sehr oft täuscht, so daß insbesondere dem Großstädter der gesunde Instinkt für artgemäße Musik abhanden gekommen ist.

Neben neuen Tanzformen stehen aus alter deutscher Kulturzeit die schönen Tanzweisen und Tanzformen unserer Eltern und Voreltern, von denen sich vor allem der Walzer auch in unsere Zeit hinübergerettet hat. Wenn auch er sich einige Wandlungen gefallen lassen mußte, so ist es die natürliche Folge davon, daß auch der ganze Lebensrhythmus der Meschen von heute sich wesentlich verändert hat gegenüber der Zeit eines Johann Strauß, Lanner, und wie sie alle heißen. Jede Zeit wird entsprechend dem Lebensrhythmus ihrer Menschen andere Tanzformen bringen. Es wäre daher wohl kaum ein erfolgreiches Experiment, wollten wir die Menschen des 20. Jahrhunderts ausschließlich auf Tanzformen aus der behäbigen Biedermeierzeit festlegen.

Typical contemporary
propaganda piece

3
The Ghetto Swingers

A thick mist delayed me, and despite Otto Jung's map I arrived on the wrong side of the Rhine from his town, Rüdesheim, near Frankfurt. The tiny car ferry crawled. The German penchant for punctuality made me jumpy. Otto had invited me for the weekend, clearing his calendar though we had never met, and I did not want to appear ungrateful.

I could barely make out the banks. Frequent mist slows Germany down. You can touch the mist, it touches you like a facecloth. But there's a rub. The mist keeps secrets. Germany has many secrets to keep; better not see too clearly. Years ago, driving north on the autobahn from Munich, the mist lifted at dawn as I passed the sign, just another autobahn exit: 'Dachau'. You miss the mist when it lifts.

There is something reassuring about coming out of the mist into a dry, hushed German cafe, like a secret hideaway. So much softer, if less gay, than a percussive Parisian bistro. Tinkling china, elderly ladies cutting cakes for their grandchildren, daily papers clamped on wooden racks. An evolved culture pleading for sympathy, given reluctantly. The waitress, a small woman with a big face, would not take money for my telephone call to Otto for directions.

Otto Jung's street address consists only of the name Boosenburg, a big house in a small town. The jolly trombonist Spiegel Wilcox, one of the last survivors of the Paul Whiteman orchestra, once mailed a letter from upstate New York addressed simply: 'To Otto who lives a stone's throw from the Rüdesheim post office in Germany' (in English) and it arrived.

The imposing structure is three-storeyed and square; its adjoining vineyard slopes to the Rhine. From outside, Boosenburg looks austere and even haunted, like a Charles Addams house; though the inside is clean, modernized with respect for the past, anything but spooky.

Thin, reserved, moving with grace, Otto led me through a series of tasteful salons. We passed two grand pianos, a violin case against a wall. He plays Mozart transcribed for four hands and string quartets with friends in the evening. This is the Germany of Beethoven and Thomas Mann. It can be described as aristocratic.

There were Germans who disapproved of Hitler not for his policies, but because he was low-class. Some older working-class Germans still resent Count Claus von Stauffenberg's circle of noble Prussian officers, who failed in their plot to murder Hitler, for being snobs who 'stabbed Germany in the back'. On the other hand, German intellectuals who oppose deployment of American nuclear missiles compare their 'resistance' to von Stauffenberg's resistance to Hitler. But a recent poll found that only thirty per cent of West Germans between the ages of sixteen and twenty-nine know anything at all about any plot in July 1944. Another German secret.

When he became a serious jazz fan in 1938, teenager Otto Jung began to resent the vocals on records he collected. Singers took time away from the real thing. He was isolated in Rüdesheim; nobody cared about the real thing, there was nobody to talk to. He wrote the Elektrola company in Berlin asking for a list of strictly instrumental Benny Goodman records.

The company could not answer his question, but they passed the letter along to Berliner Hans Bluthner, another young purist who did not like singers for the same reason. Hans made the list, mailed it; they corresponded and they remain close friends today.

After the war, when Otto's wife gave birth to a son, Hans suggested the name Lester – Lester Jung.

Hans was waiting for us on a sofa in front of a view of the misty Rhine. Unlike Otto, Hans is retired (from the construction business). He recently moved from Berlin to the nearby town of Hemsbach to be closer to his son and grandchildren. At the same time, relaxing in Boosenburg, for years a regular event, has become more convenient. The two old friends still listen to records together – old records, or new records in old styles. They listen for hours, in silence, sometimes checking personnel. Otto's record collection is indexed and cross-referenced in a looseleaf notebook. The outgoing, heavy-set and ruddy Hans completes a sort of Saxon Laurel and Hardy duo with Otto. They often laugh, but would both seem undressed in anything but suits and ties.

'You are the first person from the outside to be interested in this subject.' Hans rose to shake hands. 'Why do you suppose that is? We are so pleased you have come.'

You know jazz musicians. Heads in clouds, always late, unreliable. They had been worried I might change plans without informing them, might not show up at all. Disappointed rather than insulted by my tardiness, they were eager, hungry to talk about their youth, to reveal secret benevolence in that evil time and place.

German resistance to Nazism was not exactly a mass movement, though many now pledge retroactive allegiance. Older Germans jump at a chance to deny Nazi affiliations, but jazz is a powerful antidote and so let us be prepared to suspend disbelief.

'Jazz meant more than just music to us during the war,' Otto told me. 'Please don't take this out of context but, strange as it may sound, I remember it as a happy time.'

Otto Jung fell in love with Teddy Wilson in 1934. Other amateur musicians in his high school played in marching bands. Otto hated marching bands. He wondered why he was interested in what everybody else considered that crazy music. He was crazy about it, he must be crazy.

He transcribed Wilson's recorded piano solos, attempted his own tentative improvisations. His friends found it interesting that he was interested in Benny Goodman. The others figured he was either a Jew-lover or crazy.

His father was a talented pianist who chose to manage the family winery, on the property behind Boosenburg, rather than a musical career. Otto, who manages it now, listened to his father play four-handed piano pieces with a family friend, composer Paul Hindemith, a frequent dinner guest before he emigrated to America.

BRUNSWICK

GESANG

GRACE MOORE, Sopran
mit Orchesterbegleitung

A 82032	Ciribiribin, from "One Night of Love"	Dole-Pestalozza
	Funicull, Funicula	Denza

BING CROSBY
mit John Scott Trotter und seinem Orchester

A 81948	I've Got A POCKETFUL Of Dreams	Burce-Monaco
	from "Sing, you sinners"	
	Laugh And Call It Love from "Sing, you sinners"	Monaco-Burce
A 82040	Between A Kiss And A Sigh	Johnston-Burke
	Let's Tie The Old Forged-Me-Not	Gorney-Webster

THE ANDREWS SISTERS
mit Bob Crosby's Bob Cats

A 82042	Begin The Beguine, from "Jubilee"	Porter
	Long Time No See	Altman-Cavanaugh

mit Orchesterbegleitung

A 82051	Why Talk About Love? Fox-trot	Pollack-Mitchell
	from "Life Begins In College"	
	Begin The Beguine, from "Jubilee"	Cole Porter

THE MILLS BROTHERS

A 82033	Mr. Paganini	Lambert-Richards
	Star Dust	Carmichael-Mitchell-Parl

INSTRUMENTAL

CHARLIE KUNZ, Piano

A 82036	Charlie Kunz, Schlagerpotpourri No. 25	
	Inhalt: Deep in a dream - To mother with love - Romany - Mexicali Rose - I shall always remember you smiling - Tears on my pillow	
A 81992	Meister-Melodien No. 2	Kern
	Intro: Smoke gets in your eyes - Make believe - Dancing time - Lovely to look at - Ol' man river - Who?	
A 82038	Meister-Melodien No. 3	Rudolph Friml
	Intro: Rose Marie - Indian Love Call - The Donkey Serenade - Sympathy - Love Everlasting - Giannina Mia	

TANZMUSIK

JIMMY DORSEY ORCHESTER
mit englischem Refraingesang

A 82046	Let's Stop The Clock, Fox-trot	Coots-Gillespie
	Deep Purple, Fox-trot	de Rose-Parish

AMBROSE UND SEIN TANZ-ORCHESTER
mit englischem Refraingesang

A 82060	Deep Purple, Slow Fox-trot	Parish-De Rose
	Sixty Seconds Got Together, Slow Foxtrot	David-Livingston

A 82035	Hurry Home, Slow Fox-trot	Meyer-Bernier-Emmerich
	I Promise You, Slow Fox-trot	Lerner-Oakland-Faye
A 82037	To Mother-With Love, Slow Fox-trot	Watson-Denby-Lynton
	Sweethearts, Waltz from the Film	Herbert-Stothart-Wright-Forrest

AMBROSE UND SEIN TANZ-ORCHESTER

| A 82050 | Ah! Sweet Mystery Of Live, Quick-step | Herbert |
| | Deep Henderson | Rose |

BILLIE HOLIDAY UND IHR ORCHESTER
mit englischem Gesang

A 81918	I'VE Got A Date With A Dream, Fox-trot Tempo	Gordon-Revel
	from "My Lucky Star"	
	You Can't Be Mine (And Someone Else's Too), Fox-trot Tempo	Johnson-Webb

GENE KRUPA ORCHESTER
mit englischem Refraingesang

A 81939	Jeepers Creepers, Fox-trot	
	from "Going Places"	Mercer-Warren
	Say It With A Kiss, Fox-trot	Mercer-Warren
	from "Going Places"	

TEDDY WILSON MIT SEINEM ORCHESTER
mit englischem Refraingesang

A 81934	Let's Dream In The Moonlight, Fox-trot	Walsh-Malneck
	from "St. Louis Blues"	
	You're So Desirable, Fox-trot	Ray Noble

Juli-August
1939

BRUNSWICK
REG TRADE MARK

Preise der Platten:

25 cm . . . . RM 2,50
30 cm . . . . RM 4,25
Sonderklasse RM 3,50

THE CHAMPAGNE MUSIK OF LAWRENCE WELK

| A 81935 | Emaline, Fox-trot | Parish-Perkins |
| | That's A Plenty, Fox-trot | Pollack |

HORACE HEIDT AND HIS MUSICAL KNIGHTS
mit englischem Refraingesang

A 82048	Penny Serenade, Fox-trot	Halifax-Weersma
	Never Again, Fox-trot	Coward
	from "Set To Music"	

> *Wir spielen Ihnen gern jede Platte vor!*

G 779 Do3 S

German Brunswick catalogue, 1939

Their maid denounced Otto's father for listening to foreign radio stations, and she told the Gestapo that Jewish musicians frequented the house. When the Gestapo asked him about it, he said he was interested only in the music, he did not care about politics; but a weakness for Felix Mendelssohn cost Otto's father four months in jail.

Otto listened to jazz records on the sly, copying solos and arrangements. Neither parents nor teacher approved. But after hearing his transcription of a Herman Chittison piano solo, the teacher, who was a close friend of Hindemith and performed his works in public, made a pact with Otto. He could play Hindemith and Chittison too. She was beginning to appreciate the life-affirmation in jazz, rough-and-tumble as it was. And anything the Nazis hated could not be all bad.

A fourteen-year-old Frankfurter named Horst Lippman, now a concert promoter, played jazz records for the customers in his father's restaurant. Young fans began to gather there. Otto listened along with the others, including some impressed foreign labourers. After jazz was banned and current releases taken off the market, they continued listening to the old records and ordered new ones from France.

In 1941, they formed the Hot Club of Frankfurt. They wore blue shirts and white ties. There were gang fights with Hitler Youth in their brown and black. Club members served occasional jail sentences for delinquency.

'In America, the acceptance of jazz was a social problem, black or white,' Otto explained. 'But here it was a political problem because everybody knew the Nazis did not like jazz and wanted to suppress it. That made us love it even more. We always felt that only people who were opposed to the Nazi regime could like this music.'

'Yes yes . . .' Hans has more trouble with English than Otto, who speaks fluently, and he groped for words. 'There was a joke we told, cautiously, during Hitler times. It was a sort of fairy tale. The good fairy gave three attributes to the Germans. Honesty, intelligence and National Socialism. Everybody had these three attributes. But then came the bad fairy. She took away one of them from each person. Thereafter we had three categories of people here. First, those who were intelligent and National Socialists, but they were not honest. Second, there were honest people who were National

Socialists, but they were not intelligent. And honest, intelligent people could not be National Socialists.'

Hans' high-school friends in Berlin would say something like: 'Oh, I heard a beautiful song yesterday. Do you know it?' Humming a few bars would be enough. ' "After You've Gone",' he'd answer, playing it if a piano was around. Hans knew all the hits from the sheet music in Alberti's music store, where you could try out as many as you liked before buying one. Alberti's customers traded sheet music with each other, and he subscribed to the *Melody Maker*, which printed four lead sheets a month. 'I was the hit expert,' Hans laughed again. 'They called me "Herr Hitman".'

A Turkish friend who could 'play guitar like Eddie Lang' asked him if he'd ever heard Louis Armstrong. 'No? Oh, I will play you some records.' After hearing Armstrong, Red Nichols, Frankie Trumbauer, Duke Ellington and others, Hans lost interest in hits.

With Hitler in power, jazz records became more difficult to find. Though no fan, Alberti sensed a market for the music and asked Hans to help him stock a jazz department in the cellar of the store. Elektrola continued releasing Fats Waller records because nobody seemed to know he was black.

Hans stumbled on a new release: 'Clementine' on one side and 'Pretty Girl' on the other, by 'Jean and His Orchestra'. It had wonderful solos; he recognized Bix Beiderbecke and Joe Venuti. It must be Jean Goldkette. Goldkette is a Jewish name so the company just dropped it. He told his friends and they bought the record from Alberti.

The Berlin Hot Club was formed in 1934, the same year that Otto Jung fell in love with Teddy Wilson. Francis Wolff, who later co-founded Blue Note Records in New York, already knew about Jelly Roll Morton, Benny Moten and McKinney's Cotton Pickers. Wolff, Hans and thirty or so others met to listen to records in the back room of a cafe once a week: 'We called it the "Blue Room". Every new Hot Club member had to list his collection to prove he was really a fan. My first time, I brought a Jimmie Lunceford record nobody knew.

'We gathered around the gramophone. I remember one record had no information on the label other than "Ted Lewis and His Orchestra". The company did not think anybody cared. So we listened. Oh . . .' Hans cupped his hand like an ear trumpet.

'Who is that piano player? I have heard him somewhere.'

'It must be Fats Waller.'
'The trumpet player is Muggsy Spanier.'
'Benny Goodman on clarinet.'
Hans perched eagerly on the edge of the sofa: 'We worked it out together. I am absolutely sure there were no Nazis in the Berlin Hot Club. We always said that anybody who liked jazz could never be a Nazi.'

Before leaving to run some errands, Otto handed me a copy of Eric Vogel's article 'Jazz in a Nazi Concentration Camp', from a 1961 *Down Beat* magazine. I read it while Hans took a nap.

In 1938, Vogel played trumpet in a dixieland combo with the Paszkus brothers on guitar and drums, Bramer on piano, and Kolek clarinet. They worked semi-pro jobs around Brno, Czechoslovakia, and Vogel had one of the largest collections of jazz records in the country. He was proud to know enough English to read the occasional issue of *Down Beat* which came his way. They were too involved with jazz to worry about politics.

When the Germans invaded on 15 March 1939, the doorbells of Jews began to ring: 'Gestapo!' Vogel's turn came: '*Aufmachen!*' The man standing there in an SS uniform and a swastika on his arm had been listening to one of their jam sessions a few weeks earlier. 'Oh it's you,' he said. 'Well don't worry.'

Vogel lost his engineering job to a Christian. He continued to sell arrangements to Bobek Bryen's band. Some he transcribed from American records, Chick Webb's 'Squeeze Me' for example. Soon Jews were banned from theatres, movies, coffee houses and nightclubs and an 8 p.m. curfew was announced. So much for live music.

Vogel wore a yellow star on his lapel. The Jews of Brno were crowded into a ghetto. When his family was forced to share a two-room apartment with two other families, he practised trumpet, muted in a closet, and continued arranging. Rehearsing the Bryen band one evening, he discovered it was one hour past curfew when two Gestapo officers arrested him in the middle of 'Boogie Woogie Blues'.

They took him to headquarters. By chance his SS friend from the jam session was there. 'I have a personal account to settle with this pig Jew,' he said to his colleagues. 'Leave him to me.' This may seem cockeyed, but Vogel says the officer then took him home, borrowed some jazz records and books about jazz music and that was the end of it.

When the Nazis confiscated Jewish-owned musical instruments, Vogel soaked his valves in sulphuric acid to keep anybody from playing military marches on a jazz trumpet. Arranging was impossible without a piano.

He worked registering Czech Jews in a 'technical bureau' until – he never could figure this out – he was ordered to organize a jazz course. Not asked, not permitted – ordered. He recruited a teaching staff. Forty students applied. Waiting for instruments, the teachers gave courses in jazz theory and history. He managed to get hold of twelve recordings of 'St Louis Blues', played by twelve different groups, to illustrate how spontaneous interpretation counts more than composition. Every improviser is a composer, he said. He compared jazz musicians to painters, who are free to fill the canvas with subjective visions; while classical musicians, like photographers, must always shoot in focus.

Most of the pupils were elderly classical string players who had to be retrained on reeds and brass. After several weeks, the ensemble sounded better than he expected. It was time to find a name. He had liked the expression 'killer diller' he once found in *Down Beat*, though he had no idea what it meant. Since the name of his Jewish community was Kehila, he called his band the 'Kille Dillers'.

A thousand Jews were being shipped to unknown destinations every two weeks and on 25 March 1942, it was the Kille Dillers' turn: 'You may take with you not more than thirty pounds of baggage.' Machine-guns covered them as they boarded a waiting train. When the morning sun rose they were surprised to discover they were headed west, not east. They were prodded from the station to Theresienstadt by a pack of armed, snarling men.

Theresienstadt was an old fortress surrounded by a deep moat with a population of about 3,000 civilians plus a few thousand soldiers. The civilians were evacuated, the town sealed by a heavy guard. He met some musicians from Prague but there were no instruments so 'the only music was vocal'.

Wait a minute. It is impossible to let that go by. What did they sing? 'Blue and Sentimental'? 'Nobody Loves You when You're Down and Out'? This tale was getting hairy. I lost my first kilo.

When I wrote an article about the Kille Dillers for *Jazzistique* magazine, my translator Claude Verses called to say: 'Get someone else to translate it.'

Claude is a black American with a mother from Martinique; he translates in both directions. We are friends. He was not friendly: 'The subject is a downer. I'm sorry, man, but I can't deal with jazz in a Nazi ghetto. You think that's funny or something? I already know too much old Kraut shit. As a matter of fact I know too much new Kraut shit. You been to Germany recently? You seen what Germany done to Blow Black? Bad news, Jim. Why do you want to go write a book like this for anyway?'

'What do you mean why?' I'm afraid I shouted. 'It interests me, that's why.'

Maybe Verses was right; this is a downer. At least you can skip if you like; I've got to read between the lines and phrase precise prose. Vogel's style is so skeletal, there's so much to imagine. I long for mist.

They discovered a battered piano in an attic, some old horns were smuggled in. They played muted because entertainment was banned. Then, suddenly, it was not only permitted, but ordered. A committee for 'entertainment in your free time' (Freizeitgestaltung) was formed. The Germans were renovating Theresienstadt into a model ghetto to disprove rumours about slave labour and gas chambers. A Red Cross committee was expected.

All surfaces received a fresh coat of paint. New musical instruments arrived, ensembles were organized. Some of the best musicians in Europe were in that ghetto. On 8 January 1943, Vogel wrote a letter to the Freizeitgestaltung asking permission to start a jazz band called the Ghetto Swingers. Permission was granted.

Clarinettist Fritz Weiss, 'without any doubt one of the best jazz musicians of pre-war Europe', could also arrange and soon there was a library of twenty arrangements. Musical staves had to be drawn by hand on blank paper. Vogel taped five pencils together to save time. He arranged the band's theme song: 'I Got Rhythm'. Still basically an amateur with little reading experience, having trouble keeping up, Vogel was 'politely asked to play third trumpet and not too loudly'.

Martin Roman, once pianist with the famous Marek Weber band, was appointed leader. Vogel writes:

The Ghetto Swingers was quite a good band. We played with swing and feeling, mostly in the style of Benny Goodman. Closing my eyes now, I can almost hear Goodman emanating from Weiss' clarinet. There was Nettl, piano; Schuman, drums; Goldschmidt, guitar; Lubensky, bass; Vodnansky, alto saxophone; Donde, tenor saxophone; Kohn, Chokkes and Vogel trumpets; Taussig, trombone and Weiss on clarinet.

A guitar player named Vicherek had recently been convicted of having 'defiled musical culture' by singing Louis Armstrong's scat vocal on 'Tiger Rag' in public. And yet here the Ghetto Swingers were playing the same music in the same sort of camp to which Vicherek had been sent for playing it outside.

When the Red Cross commission (two Danes, one Swiss) arrived, the symphony orchestra played in the main square and the Ghetto Swingers were swinging in the cafe. Handed sardines, under-nourished children were ordered to complain: 'Oh, not sardines again.'

A movie was shot to document the 'good life' in Theresienstadt. The Ghetto Swingers appear several times. The film crew from Prague was impressed with the band and the band was flattered. The film includes sporting events, concerts and vaudeville and took several weeks to shoot. The band began to believe the propaganda. Perhaps the swinging, intense music they were playing had something to do with it. The carefully orchestrated Nazi illusion of freedom and security in Theresienstadt took the form of reality in their minds. They planned for the post-war future, when they would stay together and tour the world.

As soon as the Red Cross and the film crew left, on 28 September 1944, the Ghetto Swingers went on the road to Auschwitz. Fritz Weiss was gassed upon arrival: '. . . our beloved and wonderfully gifted Fritz Weiss, one of the best jazz musicians Europe ever had'.

From photographs, Fritz Weiss appears to resemble Artie Shaw more than Goodman. He is handsome and virile and you can guess from his engaged stance and determined embouchure that he probably played well. The Ghetto Swingers are on a bandstand in a park, wearing white shirts and neat neckties. It resembles a summer jazz festival.

As I write, this is the weekend of 14 July, Bastille Day, 1984. There are jazz festivals all over Europe at this time of year. Like most Parisians, my wife and child are in the country. The telephone is silent; I have been writing night and day for two days in my tiny *chambre de bonne*.

Today's *Herald Tribune* ran a story about James Oliver Huberty, who shot twenty-one people in a McDonald's restaurant in San Ysidro, California. 'Where are you going, honey?' Mrs Huberty had asked when her husband came to kiss her goodbye. 'Human hunting,' he replied.

I am fed up with suffering and death; my back hurts, my eyes ache. Sore and morose, lonely, in dire need of some swing, I wonder what the attempt to construct graceful prose has to do with any of this, but I promised myself three solid days' work and they are not over yet.

In Auschwitz, Vogel was pushed towards a hill. An SS officer on top pointed either left or right. Waiting at the bottom, an elderly guard asked Vogel: 'What did you do in Theresienstadt?'

'I played in a jazz band.'

'Just what we need here. When you come to the top of the hill tell the officer you are in perfect health and take ten years off your age.'

Vogel went left; the gas chambers were to the right. Before falling asleep in the barracks he watched a Dutch Jew who had finked on other Jews tortured to a slow death by inmates. The next day, the prisoners were ordered outside to be counted. They stood foodless for hours in a snowstorm. The weak passed out or were led away. Vogel was beaten by young trustees in striped pyjamas.

After an SS man commanded: '*Musiker, vortreten*', (musicians, step forward), he punched Vogel in the stomach for the hell of it and said follow me. In barracks two, Vogel was astonished to find several surviving Ghetto Swingers. They embraced and kissed. In a few hours he was dressed in a sharp band uniform. He had shoes, food, cigarettes. He was introduced to 'the two German mass-murderers' who were in charge of the camp, one of whom, Willy, asked what instrument he played.

'Trumpet.'

'We already have two,' Willy groaned.

Vogel froze; he knew the price of redundancy in these places.

But Willy was a music lover: 'I'll get you a trumpet even if I have to sell a bottle of whisky for it.'

Thirty musicians played symphonies, operas and jazz without written music twelve hours a day for the guards, one of whom said: 'You guys are good. There was a wonderful Gypsy band here for six weeks. They were good too but they went up the chimney.'

Vogel writes: 'We had some good players among us and we made good music' – until leaving, by freight train not chimney, four weeks later. 'During the voyage, we sang local versions of the music we had been playing, like Lambert–Hendricks–Ross would do later.'

Arriving in the Heinkel aircraft factory, which was running low on slaves, somebody told an officer: 'We are musicians. We were in the Auschwitz choir.' He was beaten; music was not mentioned again, though an inspector who remembered Martin Roman from the Marek Weber band did what he could to ease their workload.

Vogel jumped off a gondola car headed for the final solution in Dachau and managed to reach the forest. He was starving and the Allies were close so he took a chance crawling out when he saw an automobile. Nuts! Luftwaffe officers. But they knew they were soon going to need all the good karma they could get and they gave him bread and directions to the nearby village of Petzenhausen, where he was fed hot black coffee and potatoes and hidden in a barn.

He rubbed his eyes in disbelief when he saw what was printed in large letters on the side of the first American jeep to enter the village: 'BOOGIE WOOGIE'.

4
Doctor Jazz

If nobody who liked jazz could be a Nazi, what about all those guards and SS men?

The answer goes something like this. These people were not necessarily jazz fans. They liked swing, the popular dance music of the day. Swing can either be a style of music or of life. Swing, the music, was not necessarily jazz, though it often involved a 'hot break' or improvisation in the middle somewhere. Swing bands did not threaten the regime; the good ones were rather regimented themselves. Precision was essential in a good swing band. Defined as a lifestyle, swing can simply mean fun. Some people have funny fun. Nazis swung beating people up. The swing style of popular music was basically for dancing, a popular way to have fun. Nazis danced to swing until their defeat at Stalingrad when Goebbels banned it. Fun was never against the law.

During Otto Jung's compulsory pre-military service: working in the fields, building walls, cleaning parks, helping little old ladies across the street, he played swing records over the PA system in the mess hall. Hans sent Otto the list of instrumental Benny Goodman records about that time. When nobody was around he improvised on the recreation-room piano. A drummer in a Hitler Youth marching band liked to improvise too and sometimes they played together.

Luftwaffe ace Werner Molders, a swing fan, would switch on the BBC as he crossed the Channel, hoping to catch a few bars of Glenn Miller before bombing the antenna. Hitler had a weak spot for his pilots. When Molders complained about the unswinging music on German radio, Hitler spoke to Goebbels about it. This led to the establishment of a Berlin radio house band called Charly and His

Orchestra, which tried for a while to send out swinging signals to the world.

If anybody who loved jazz could not be a Nazi, there seem to have been quite a few close calls. If a love for jazz in general precludes racism, what about Crow Jim today? Why do so many violent movies have jazz-oriented soundtracks if jazz and violence don't go together? When a jazz musician is stoned, he is 'bombed'. When he plays hot, he's 'smoking'. Why these action-packed adjectives for such a non-violent segment of humanity? Is it cynical to ask if it isn't a bit convenient for elderly German jazz fans to say that anybody who loved jazz could not be a Nazi?

Europe was bombed and smoking in 1944, when the bottle of brandy Otto was opening had been distilled by his company. We marvelled at the label. 'Did your company make a profit in 1944?' I asked him, but he was called out of the room for an overseas call. Forty years later, Jung's wine exports to America are healthy.

'We had more liberty to avoid the regulations in Berlin than Frankfurt,' said Hans. 'They wanted to offer foreigners cosmopolitan entertainment. We had friends who would warn us that today will come an inspector from the Nazi Musicians' Association and then the band played less hot. They played the Moonlight Sonata, they gave the songs another title in German. Not translations, just any old thing. These Nazis didn't know anything. They believed what they were told. They were so silly. One day somebody came from the Musicians' Association and told the band to play more hot. He liked it hot.'

Otto returned and said: 'They called jazz "*Entartete*", which means not in conformity with the pure German character. That is a strange concept, no? Purity. But if I had to choose I would prefer pure *African* character . . .'

'Just Asking', an article by Martin Williams in *Jazz Times*:

Putting it in terms of my generation; why would it be that a young man growing up in Chicago in the teens of this century, the son of Russian Jewish emigrant parents, would want to learn to play the clarinet like a coloured creole from New Orleans named Jimmie Noone? Why would the act of doing this be so meaningful to him? And having done that, why would he then want to form an orchestra that played like that of an American mulatto from Georgia named Fletcher Henderson? And stake his career in music on doing that? And after he had done that, why would the world make him a celebrity and one of the most famous musicians of the century?

I write of course of Benny Goodman.

Let me put essentially the same question in terms of a later generation. Why would it be that a skinny kid from London, an economics student, would want to try to sing like a relatively ignorant black man from Mississippi? Why would that be so meaningful to him? And having done as best he could, why would the world make him a star, a sex symbol, and a millionaire? And why would audiences want to watch him sing on stages in huge auditoriums in a lamé jump suit with on occasion (I'm told) a padded codpiece?

I write of course of Mick Jagger.

Why do we all, at whatever level, find such meaning in the musical culture of Afro-Americans? Why has their music so triumphed throughout the world? We invoke it to get through our adolescence and most of us keep it, one way or another, central in our lives . . .

Just asking. Am I missed? I am missing. After fifteen years of expatriatism, I miss the Afro-American swing of New York streets. It had been central in my life. It may have triumphed throughout the world but it gets into French heads, not under their skin. It has not triumphed in France.

Moving to Paris had never been a conscious decision. I consider myself on permanent loan, like a Picasso. One year led to another and now I find myself without a place to hang. 'Profit,' Henry James wrote to Edith Wharton, 'by my awful example of exile and ignorance. Do New York.'

Too late. New York is done with me. I am hung. Parisian loneliness has become literally breathtaking, a gasp not a gas. There are times when I hate the French with great passion; but then it turns into, if not love, a marriage of convenience. Today's *Herald Tribune* carried a story about a visitor who complained that he had not seen the coral snake budge in nine months of visits to the Houston Zoo. Curator John Donaho replied: 'Snakes on exhibit tend to die, so we put out a rubber one.'

America has promoted ersatz into something to shoot for rather than put up with. America is a phoney fire made by a gas jet burning behind fake logs in a plastic fireplace. One big unkept promise. The preference for African culture by people like Otto Jung is what keeps me in Europe. He continued: '... Hitler promised a thousand-year Reich covered with glory. He said to work, be strong, fight for the fatherland. During the depression years, while one out of three workers was unemployed, there had been what they called this Jewish decadent culture that dominated music, theatre, all the arts. Hitler said this is not compatible with Aryan culture. Military marches were played continually. German people like military music. Jazz represented the other way, the weak way. People who listened to jazz were regarded as opposed to the regime.

'I suppose ...' Otto hesitated: 'I suppose Schulz-Koehn was not as opposed as we were.'

Hans nodded, thoughtful, tentative: 'I wonder ...'

'But you must remember, his father was a Nazi.'

'Terrible.'

'His father was a party member, a teacher. Many teachers followed the Nazis, especially at the beginning. Schulz-Koehn grew up in a house where they were talking in favour of these things, in Magdeburg. It was not that he approved. He just did not want to see the bad side. I remember one night in January, 1943 ...'

Jazz veterans of the Third Reich tend to remember forty-year-old dates and locations as though they were yesterday: '...He came to see me in Frankfurt. I was a student. I invited my jazz friends and we discussed until 3 a.m. We all agreed that we would have to lose the war to be able to keep jazz alive. "If Hitler wins the war, jazz is finished," that's what we told him. He did not see it that way. He said, "You know, I am in uniform, here I have my picture taken with Django, with a Gypsy and coloured musicians and everything is fine." He said, "Look, I have no difficulty."'

Hans added: 'He was the only one in our small circle of jazz people who did not want to acknowledge what was happening in Germany. He *behaved* like an anti-Nazi but when you talked to him ... well, it was schizophrenic. He wrote articles in our secret newsletter; the first issue had his photograph in uniform on the first page. If some official had bothered to notice, he would have gone to jail immediately. He did a lot of good. He took a lot of risks.'

Otto wondered if perhaps Schulz-Koehn printed his photo in uniform in the newsletter not out of youthful innocence but to protect his friends who were working on it – to lend it a sort of first-view official aura. Schulz-Koehn remains friends with Charles Delaunay, then Secretary-General of the Hot Club de France, who confirms that he distributed ration cards and clandestine letters whenever he passed through their rue Chaptal headquarters in Pigalle. Delaunay calls him 'an honest and gentle man. As far from racist as you can get.'

Flash 150 kilometres north-west to Liblar, near Cologne, to meet Dietrich Schulz-Koehn, the German officer who loved the Count: 'All I am or own was made possible by jazz. If I hadn't been so keen on it, perhaps I would have remained as stubborn as the Nazis. Jazz opened my mind.'

It had begun as a love affair like the others. That first fatal blast of swing followed by close listening, analysis and discussion. Here however, the affair became a marriage as he found a market for his expertise. When the war broke out, Schulz-Koehn was working for Telefunken Records: 'Now you would call it marketing.' With his knowledge of English and French, he supervised their editions in these languages. He built a name producing jazz for Elektrola, Deutsche Grammophon and Brunswick Records. He wrote under the pen-name 'Swing Doc'.

Then he was mobilized: 'I belonged to the Luftwaffe but as I wear spectacles I stayed on the ground. We had to defend the airports against parachutists, we would be transferred often to new assignments.'

His staccato, enthusiastic phrases have long, weary pauses between them. The opportunity to explain himself seems to be providing a shot of youth. He obviously feels the need to prove something to people – including myself maybe – who will not sympathize with any Luftwaffe officer, even a Count Basie fan.

'A small Belgian company had recorded two sides of Django Reinhardt playing the violin, very rare. They are out of print now I think. I had copies with me always, and in Nîmes I was asked to play them over the radio. So imagine, here I was sitting in full uniform in front of the microphone in the studio in Nîmes, a German officer telling French jazz fans about Django Reinhardt.'

In 1936 Schulz-Koehn had been in a London studio when Django cut six sides. Freddy Taylor sang on several. When Taylor heard that 'Georgia on My Mind' would be among them, he groaned: 'I don't know the lyrics.' Schulz-Koehn sat in a corner and wrote them down. Glancing at Django, who was wearing an expensive Stetson hat, he spotted a sock through a torn sole. And when Django lifted his left hand to tune his guitar, a ripped sleeve seam could be seen. This did not diminish the German's respect for the Gypsy . . . on the contrary.

A Gypsy jazz musician, Django is the only non-American jazz musician to have spawned a school. Jazz musicians have some outlaw in them somewhere if they are serious about this music. Gypsies are defined as outlaws by society. So during World War II, here was a double outlaw on the lam from a regime which considered jazz musicians monkeys and shipped Gypsies to unspeakable places.

When a musician decides to play jazz for a living, he automatically becomes an outlaw. There is no valid motivation for it other than love – outlaw motivation in a profit-motivated society. He leaves the crowd. It is not a worn path. There are brambles everywhere. It takes a hard skin, good nerves, a stout heart and psychological balance. Not everyone can hack wilderness. Improvisers tend to transpose musical values to a life-view. Eschew insurance and don't vote. Those who create the 'sound of surprise' for a living are not likely to plan very far ahead. Decide what to do today today. We are unreliable, make abrupt turns on short notice. There are exceptions, of course, but Django was not one of them.

Yet he eased through the occupation checking into the best hotels, riding in limousines, gambling for high stakes, eating gourmet food, sleeping until mid-afternoon. His picture on the walls of Paris, his concerts all sold-out; French and Germans alike whistled his song 'Nuages' (Clouds) in the street. But he played billiards or went fishing if he did not feel like performing, contract notwithstanding, disappeared on the road for months with his Gypsy brothers. He was free as a monkey swinging from high trees, above the rules, like a secret agent, a double agent so confident that he could afford to come out from deep cover and have his picture taken with a Luftwaffe officer.

Dietrich Schulz-Koehn pulled out a small, neatly folded piece of paper with scribbling on it. 'I have something here which is very dear to me. In 1959 a cartoonist from Berlin was in Marseille and he happened to go into a bistro that had only jazz on the juke box. A young man from Africa working there asked him, "Are you from Germany? Yes? Do you know Dietrich Schulz-Koehn?" The cartoonist said yes, through my broadcasts. The African had heard my programme from Nîmes and he said it had been very important to him. Can you imagine? It had made such a deep impression on him. He wrote this note to me, "In the name of all jazz fans who know what you have done for jazz during the war, thank you . . ." '

Schulz-Koehn's request for a Count Basie record in Brittany was treated as a laughing matter in a *Saturday Evening Post* article titled '100,000 Nazi Clowns on the Zany Front' by Collie Small:

> . . . At this point, enter Oberleutnant Schulz-Koehn, greatcoat flapping at his ankles, the enemy jazz fiend. I stopped him and said, 'You look worried, Schulz-Koehn.'
>
> He peered at me through his horn-rimmed glasses. 'No,' he said thoughtfully. 'No, I'm not worried.' Then he added, 'Are you?'
>
> This surprised me a little, and I said 'No.' Then I said, just to brighten up Schulz-Koehn's day, 'Lieutenant Wessman and I are just in a hurry to leave here so we can drive back to Nantes and have one of those big steaks at Mainguy's restaurant.' Schulz-Koehn looked as though his stomach had jumped into his throat, but he only glared. 'I hear there is a fine jazz band there now,' I said.
>
> Schulz-Koehn's gnomelike face lit up. 'How is it?' he asked excitedly. I couldn't answer that because I had never been to Mainguy's in my life, and I was reasonably sure the band existed only in my imagination. But I told Schulz-Koehn it was very hot.
>
> 'I'll have to latch on to that some time,' he said. Then he smiled. 'You know, I asked an American officer a week ago what "latch on" meant, and he didn't know. I thought you were all jazz fans.'
>
> . . . Major Parr looked at his watch. 'Say, we'd better get out of here. The war starts again in ten minutes.'

Returning from what he calls 'my prisonership', Schulz-Koehn

16. Juli 1936   „Das Schwarze Korps"

„Swing-swing, lieb' Mütterlein...!"

Das neueste, wo man hat, ist: Swing-Musik. Was das ist, konnten wir nicht in Erfahrung bringen. Jedenfalls war (nach Ansicht der Firma Brunswick) Duke Ellington die letzten Wochen Gegenstand erregtester Diskussionen. Ja, manche glaubten schon das Ende Dukes für die Swing-Musik zu sehen, aber die Befürchtung, daß der kultivierteste Vertreter des Swings für diesen verloren sei, waren Gott sei Dank, wie uns seine Platte „Good night, Pepi" zeigt, grundlos! —

Auch war es nicht anders zu erwarten, daß Armstrong das Triumphlied des Swings „Harlem-Baby" singen würde. Das Geheimnis seines Gesanges liegt darin, daß er nicht dem Bel-Canto-Ideal nachstrebt, das wäre nicht jazzmäßig, sondern daß Armstrong seine Stimmbänder nur „belegt" schwingen läßt und sich so dem Bel-Conto-Ideal nähert. Den ungemein dunklen Klang, der seinen „Hot"-Gesang charakterisiert, erzielt er mit einer auf die Nase gesetzten Wäscheklammer.

Nun zu Chick-Webb, wohl dem reinsten Vertreter des Swings. Sein Fox „Blue Goy" besticht uns zunächst durch die meisterhaft gestopfte Trompete. Darüber hinaus arbeiten aber seine Solisten (O' Graws: singende Raslerklinge und Al Ganove: Repetierpistole) so überragend, daß der (mit der Grammophonnadel gelmpfte) Werbefritze der Brunswicks mit Recht ausrufen darf: Chick-Webb zeigt uns mit seinem Orchester echtesten „Chikago-Stil!" —

(who does not have a gnomelike face), changed his pen-name from 'Swing Doc' to 'Doctor Jazz', which is printed on his mailbox on this secure street in a quiet suburb of Cologne. Semi-retired, there are still some radio broadcasts to do, the occasional article to write, and his book *Let's Swing* – a sort of how-to-dig-it course – was published a few years ago. But there is time now, time for long walks with his two wire-haired dachshunds, time to sift through old documents, time to remember.

'Everything was saved.' He pointed to all the cartons and boxes with documents. 'Through the evacuations and the bombs. Isn't that amazing? I still have everything.'

The SS newspaper *Das Schwarze Korps* illustrated the decadence of jazz in 1936 by a drawing of old socks being blown out of a trumpet and gangsters shooting pistols. (See above.)

His Hot Club of France membership card, dated 1935; the programme for his lecture to Hot Club members in Paris in 1943; the photograph with Django in front of La Cigale: 'Amazing. Here I

Zeichnungen: Wal:.

Der Schlager dieser Season dürfte aber unzweifelhaft „The brocken Rekord" („Die gebrochene Schallplatte") sein, welche auf dem Grundsatz: „Sag ihr's mit Elektrola" basiert. Es ist wahnsinnig anheimelnd, wenn sich die Platte scheinbar immer auf derselben Stelle dreht und spielt: „Ich lieb dich, — Ich lieb dich, ich lieb . . ." (Dieselbe Platte ist auch mit dem Refrain: „Du kannst mich, du kannst mich . . . küssen, my dear of Hawai" lieferbar).

Nun, zum Schlusse, zu einem neuartigen, eigentlich jazzfremden Vertreter des Swings: Ferdy White. (Im wilden Süden auch fälschlicherweise „Weiss Ferdl" genannt). Dieser nimmt einen Leberknödel, stopft ihn aber nicht in eine Trompete, sondern in den Mund, und songt: „So long dear Old — the — Beda . . ." (Deutsch: „So lang der alte Peter . . ."). Natürlich „swingt" er hierzu — einen Maßkrug.

am in uniform with a Gypsy, four Negroes and a Jew.'

He seems to show it everywhere. I kept running into people who had seen the photo. One German musician laughed condescendingly: 'He hands them out like business cards.'

'How was it taken?' I asked Schulz-Koehn.

'Well, we came out of the club after listening and drinking and I said to a German soldier who was passing by, "Here's my camera. Take a picture of us." He said, "*Jawohl, Herr Oberleutnant.*" '

Simple. A tourist has his picture taken with the natives. Are we to assume they were being friendly? Or was subtle, even unconscious, occupational pressure involved? The occupied French were not exactly breaking down doors to have their photos taken with uniformed German officers. We are beginning to get the impression that another set of rules somehow operated in the world of jazz.

Al Lirvat, the black Guadeloupian trombonist standing next to Schulz-Koehn in the photo had not only never seen it, but did not remember it and did not consider it interesting enough to ask for a copy when I showed it to him. If it embarrassed him, he was good at hiding it.

'I knew many German musicians and jazz fans who had been in Paris before the war,' Lirvat said. 'They spoke French, now they were back as soldiers. We drank together in the cafes. We had French passports. Nobody tried to send us to the camps. I felt no racism. I never knew anybody who had any trouble for being black. I remember a cafe with a sign in the window, "No Jews or Niggers", but that was the French who did that. The French were much more racist against blacks than the Germans.'

The director of La Cigale did not want to hire black musicians because he was afraid the Germans did not like *gens de couleur*. There had been a scene in Dijon. A French woman who refused to date a German officer was later seen with a black musician. The band had been fired for that in Dijon.

The leader, a Camerounais who spoke German, complained to the German authorities that the owner of La Cigale was keeping them from working because they were black. This particular German official liked jazz; he issued a permit: 'And I can tell you that not only was there never a problem, but the Germans were happy to hear us. They applauded. We had a special authorization to play jazz. If it had been illegal, the authorities would have stopped German soldiers from coming there. We had good relations. We never talked politics, of course; we talked about the weather or music.'

Special authorization?

'Yes. We knew we were playing music that was banned, but we had it in writing. The word "jazz" was written on our permit. That's all we played. The French owners were nervous but the place was full of Germans and they didn't want trouble. There were plenty of Germans who just liked good music. We didn't go out of our way to be friendly. You never knew when you'd fall on some racist nut, but that's not all that different from now.'

Is Lirvat cool, insensitive or defensive? Why would Gypsies be sent to camps and blacks be immune? What role does Uncle Tom play in the story?

Latent prejudice against black skin in Hitler's birthplace Austria was brought to the surface in the late twenties when Josephine Baker performed there. Articles comparing Negroes to dinosaurs were printed. From *Naked at the Feast*, Lynn Haney's biography of

Baker: 'In predominantly Catholic countries, Josephine was like a red flag before the bull of the clergy-dominated political parties. "The Catholics pursued me with Christian hate," she said, "from railway station to railway station, from city to city, from one province to another." '

Nazi philosophy eventually developed a high degree of consistency and evil brilliance with its theory that all avant-garde art – Berg, Stravinsky, Picasso – was 'Negroid'. As Baker rode down the streets of Vienna, Catholic church bells rang warnings about 'the devil incarnate, the demon of immorality'. The Austrian parliament held a debate to decide whether Baker threatened public morals. Student racists hurled ammonia bombs at her, screaming: 'Go back to Africa.'

Ten years later when Hitler invaded Austria, he looked over his bed in the Weinzinger Hotel and was horrified to find himself looking at a photograph of Josephine Baker.

So Lirvat's experience must be seen in the French context. He was French, not black. The Germans were willing to look over many 'distasteful' elements of French society in return for collaboration.

There were not enough Africans in Europe for the Nazis to bother about. Lirvat could feel easy about his picture being taken with a Luftwaffe officer and converse with German soldiers because his colour and metier afforded him a certain immunity from suspicion as a collaborator. He was at the very least next in line for the camps. Anything short of finking goes in the name of survival. From his point of view, a German racist was no worse than a French one. But jazz has a key role. Django performed for Germans and was not labelled a 'collabo'; Maurice Chevalier had problems for doing basically the same thing. Jazz was outlaw music, underground by the definition of both society in general and authority in particular. All jazz musicians were German Jews.

At least one white fan did not want to be seen in the same frame with a German uniform. The Belgian critic Carlos de Radzitzky was working in his office at the coal board in 1943 when the telephone rang. The voice spoke French with a German accent – Schulz-Koehn passing through Brussels after a mission to Stockholm: 'I have a present for you. Can we meet for a coffee?'

'Pardon me, Dieter, but are you in uniform?'

There was a short silence: 'Yes.'

'Then I can't see you in public. It would be bad for my reputation.'

They made cloak-and-dagger arrangements to meet in the stockroom of a nearby record shop. Walking there, Radzitzky felt uneasy. Was it a trap? Who knew what a German officer permitted to travel to neutral Sweden might be up to?

But there were no secret documents, no microfilms, no Gestapo agents to arrest him. Only a 78 r.p.m. recording of Duke Ellington's 'Take the "A" Train', which Radzitzky had never heard.

'Thank you, Dieter,' he said, moved. 'I'm sorry, we both love jazz, but, you know, we're enemies.'

Schulz-Koehn pulled out another carton from behind his sofa: 'Ah! Look at this.' A *Saturday Review* article about a jazz band that was playing in a cellar while German troops patrolled the streets of Paris above. There were Germans (including himself) scattered among the civilians, 'clapping hands, tapping feet, nodding heads in rhythmic agreement' when suddenly the Gestapo splintered the door down and an officer barked: 'Jam sessions *sind verboten*.'

He still has a copy of the first *Melody Maker* he ever saw: August 1932; the invoice for a set of drums, dated 1929; the sheet music to 'Linger Awhile', which was the first vehicle on which his violin teacher let him improvise; an 'obituary' for jazz in a 1935 edition of a German paper: 'No more Nigger music on the radio . . .'

All these yellowed, torn pieces of paper and faded photographs. Hugues Panassié's castle in Montauban on an old post card. Schulz-Koehn had visited there (in civilian clothes) while the battle for Stalingrad was raging, to trade his brittle shellac recordings from Sweden for those Panassié managed to smuggle through Portugal and Switzerland: 'The only one he wouldn't part with on any account was "Jiving with Jarvis" by Nat King Cole and Lionel Hampton. He loved that record.'

A document from 1932, a programme for a jazz concert in the Frankfurt Conservatory: 'Mathias Seiber – have you heard of him? No? He had a jazz school in Frankfurt in the thirties. It must have been the first jazz school anywhere.

'Oh, we had such a rich cultural life before the Nazis. Can you imagine what would have happened to jazz in Germany if there had been no Hitler?'

5
Rosebud

'Oh, this is good medicine.' Hans Bluthner raised a tumbler of 1944 German brandy. 'A toast to jazz.'

If you wanted to be bitchy about it, you might describe Hans as somebody who is modest because he has a lot to be modest about. But he has only himself to blame if that is accurate. His every movement, and even the way he holds still, implies the certainty that he is, as a critic once described a novel he rather liked, 'underwhelming'. He is an average Hans who would prefer to have been an average Joe.

He did not make history, he witnessed it. He did not make music, he listened. He sat in front of bandstands, not on them. His contribution was passive – actively passive you could say: creative listening. Hans had these peculiar ears that could hear fine art in what 'normal' people, even intelligent normal people, were still calling 'primitive' and 'savage' music.

Swiss conductor Ernest Ansermet was one of the few who had already heard that; much earlier, more than fifteen years earlier. In the October 1919 issue of the *Revue Romande* he wrote an article entitled 'On a Negro Orchestra' which analysed work songs, the blues, syncopation and swing and concluded:

> . . . I am inclined to think that the strongest manifestation of the Negro racial genius lies in the blues. The blues occurs when the Negro is sad, when he is far from his home, his mammy, or his sweetheart. Then he thinks of a motif or a preferred rhythm, and takes his trombone or his violin, or his banjo, or his clarinet, or his drum, or else he sings or simply dances. And on the chosen motif he plumbs the depth of his imagination.

This makes his sadness pass away. It is the blues.

. . . There is in the Southern Syncopated Orchestra an extraordinary clarinet virtuoso who is, so it seems, the first of his race to have composed perfectly formed blues on the clarinet. I've heard two of them which he had elaborated at great length, then played to his companions so that they could make up an accompaniment. Extremely difficult, they are equally admirable for their richness of invention, force of accent and daring in novelty and the unexpected. Already they gave the idea of a style, and their form was gripping, abrupt, harsh, with a brusque and pitiless ending like that of Bach's second Branden-burg Concerto. I wish to set down the name of this artist of genius; as for myself, I shall never forget it. It is Sidney Bechet. When one has tried so often to rediscover in the past one of those figures to whom we owe the advent of our art – those men of the seventeenth and eighteenth centuries, for example, who made expressive works of dance airs, clearing the way for Haydn and Mozart, who mark not the starting point, but the first milestone – what a moving thing it is to meet this very black, fat boy with white teeth and that narrow forehead, who is very glad one likes what he does, but who can say nothing of his art save that he follows his 'own way', and then one thinks that this 'own way' is perhaps the highway the whole world will swing along tomorrow . . .

Europe was not exactly swinging along Ansermet's highway when the Third Reich arrived; it was in second gear on the ramp. And it was being driven by the likes of Hans Bluthner.

Though he resisted the Third Reich with minimal risk if any, Hans Bluthner's resistance is essential to our story just because of its underwhelming nature: 'I always said that had it not been for jazz, I would have died during the war. It gave me so much happiness and hope. It proved to me that I was not a German but a member of humanity.'

Rarely, if ever, has any art affected the lives of 'normal' human beings as directly as jazz in Nazi-occupied Europe. It was daily catharsis, a purifying release from tension. The people who played this music were sure that they were involved in *the* art form of the twentieth century. Its principal element, swing, was symbolic, pertinent and physical. Swing was the popular music of that time and place. Please note that I do not include Germany itself in this assessment; only the countries it occupied. Jazz was packed with drama, it was political dynamite, aesthetically ecological, created with religious fervour, and it was popular. A rare conjunction.

'Oh, this is a funny story,' Hans laughed. 'Panassié requested me in 1937 to find lip salve for Louis Armstrong.'

Hugues Panassié was an early convert to jazz, who wrote bibles more than books. He passed down the law rather than presented opinions. When he moved to the castle in the village of Montauban, he was called 'the Pope of Montauban'. The post-war split with Charles Delaunay, his co-founder of the Hot Club de France, over the artistic validity of bebop, was known in all seriousness as the Schism.

Hans was in Paris for the 1937 Worlds Fair, a monk on a pilgrimage. (Django Reinhardt was preaching.) Hans would never become a cardinal, he would remain a lay worker, but he felt blessed to be asked to fetch holy water for an apostle: 'Louis had trouble with chapped lips, always trouble. His lips would bleed. His favourite lip cream came from Germany. Pannassié told me the brand-name and asked if I could try and find it in Berlin.'

Returning home with a valise full of records purchased in Paris, Hans was asked by the German customs agent if there was propaganda on them. 'No. No talk, just music,' he said.

'Is that true?'

'You can play it. I'm interested only in music.'

'We don't have a gramophone. Are you sure it's music?'

'Sure.'

'Why do you buy it in Paris?'

'These do not exist in Berlin. This is special. It's dance music – tango and foxtrot.'

'What does it mean? Dance music? I'm sure there's talk here.' The customs officer banged the table: 'Show me your passport.' He looked at it: 'You're not a musician.'

'I like to play these songs on the piano. It's my hobby.'

'There's *talk*. I know it!'

The train whistle began to blow. Hans should have thought of it earlier: 'If there's an import duty I will pay.'

'Fifteen Reichmarks.'

Hans asked for Louis Armstrong's lip cream in pharmacies all over Berlin. 'Nobody knew of it. I had a talk with a trombone player who played with Teddy Stauffer and the Teddies and he said, "You must ask in a music shop." But then came the war.'

Hans had begun his working life at twenty-one, approving credit in the automobile loan department of a bank. He liked the job because the economy was booming and he liked saying yes to people. But when car production was militarized, he had no more customers. His childless uncle who owned a building firm said: 'Hans, you are the right man for me.'

They were busy building barracks and factories, 'but there was a sales manager who . . .' Hans sighed deeply, and said with a guttural moan that reminded me of a Monty Python good German: '. . . Oh, he was a bad man.'

I do not want to appear to be making fun of him; rarely have I liked a stranger as instinctively as I liked Hans Bluthner. We are so different in our age, genes and experience, but we have our ears in common. Our common love is a bond. Jazz acted as a love-force back in the times of the great hate, and it is still a Love Supreme. I would be willing to put my reputation on the line – I *am* putting it on the line – and say that if ever there was one good German it is Hans Bluthner.

'Jazz was my only pleasure in those times, in every other way they were terrible. There were all sorts of crazy people. Craziness was everywhere. I had this friend, he collected only coloured musicians. He was shocked when he heard that Jack Teagarden was not a Negro, he stopped collecting Teagarden records right away.'

A 'good German' in the Third Reich condemns Jack Teagarden for being too Aryan. That's the trouble with 'good' Germans. Hans was too sane for that, too average perhaps, but a level head is saintly where the devil rules: 'Colour did not matter to me, I either liked the music or not.'

Interested in what was happening on all fronts, Hans listened to Radio London and Moscow. He came into the office one day and said: 'The Americans bombed Düsseldorf. The war will soon be over. Then I will congratulate my Jewish friends that we have lost the war.' The sales manager wrote it down in the little book he always carried.

In 1944 the Gestapo took away his uncle, who had always

expressed interest in what Hans had heard on Radio London and Moscow. Hans was 'invited' to testify. The Gestapo quoted his uncle's every word, and his own. 'The truth,' the officer tapped the sales manager's notebooks on the table, 'is all written here.'

Hans sensed that the Gestapo officers could not understand him. It was obvious he was no threat to the system, and just as obvious that he was somehow immune from their control. He had not broken any laws and his racial credentials were impeccable, yet he must be guilty of *something*.

His odd ear seemed to be infecting the rest of his head; it was a disease more than treason. They had no cure. It had no name. It should be quarantined. He was to be pitied more than feared. The closest crime they could define was 'unpatriotic', which was bad enough, but they could not even pin that down. They asked why he wasn't a soldier. 'My arm will not bend since an old accident, and I have osteomyelitis in one leg.' He produced supporting documents.

'By this time all the camps were full, they had no more room to put people,' is how Hans explained why he stayed out of them, and why his uncle was released and returned home early.

The logic does not seem to strike him as faulty. Has he forgotten that the Nazis devised other ways to empty camps, and that overcrowding did not necessarily result in premature home leave? Like an anti-apartheid Afrikaner, he benefited from an exploitative system he disapproved of. If he ever reflected upon the nature of his luck, he has by now forgotten it. Is this very different from the rest of us? Figuratively, we calculate good deeds in terms of listening to banned music made by 'subversive' people and hope this will be enough to settle accounts in our favour. Passive good deeds, the absence of bad deeds. We have families to support.

'My son was born in 1944; we had a baby. There was no warm place to stay, nothing to eat. We spent every night and some days in the cellar during the bombings. There was no more time to listen to jazz. Everybody had to walk home from work at the end. No more public transportation. We were living at my uncle's house. By luck, it was still standing. I stored my records there. One day a man stopped at the door. He was very tired and he could not reach home that night. Could he sleep at our house? Of course. We discovered we both liked music. I asked what kind and he said, "Nothing you'd know about, a special kind of music called jazz." I grinned, "Me too." '

Hans' outrage is so guileless, what follows would be laughable if it hadn't been said with such genuine distress: 'When the Russians came, they stamped on my records. That was not necessary. I had such a wonderful collection.'

He found himself in the British zone. His uncle's firm had to be reconstructed with no Nazi executives; everybody had to be cleared. The sales manager came back looking for his old job: 'He was shy, like a boy, he talked about how much he had suffered during Nazi times.' Hans told the British that he had denounced his uncle to the Gestapo: 'The British asked him how he could say he was not a Nazi and yet he gave his notebooks to the Gestapo. He said, "It was an accident. I had them in my pocket and they took them from me." But that is not possible. No, I do not believe it.

'But then we could come into the open with German jazz. Our Hot Club had jam sessions, only members and jazz lovers. Some American soldiers. People brought instruments. They came together often without knowing each other. We made this for love not money. The musicians played only for fun. It is different today; musicians play only for money today. They have a right to be paid but I think today so much of fun has gone out of the music.

'Panassié asked me about the lip cream for Louis Armstrong again in 1948. A man in an old music shop told me, "Yes, they made it before the war. We will see if it still exists." And he found it. I sent it to Panassié and he sent it to Louis. Louis wrote me a letter; how happy he was.'

This is a fairy tale not a horror story. Nightmares lead to sweet dreams: 'Then in 1952, I heard from Panassié, "Louis will come to Berlin and you must go to the airport to meet him." He came off the plane and embraced me. He said: "Hans, Hans." '

Suddenly, like a clap of thunder, *angst* and *sturm* and *drang* arrived at Boosenburg in the form of Emil Mangesldorff and Carlo Bohlander.

Bohlander is a thin man who seems to burn off fat in front of your eyes. He was discharged from the German army by managing to get down under the weight limit of 100 pounds. His eyes burn too. He is married to an Afro-American woman who runs an attractive small cafe in the old quarter of downtown Frankfurt; he has written a German encyclopaedia of jazz, is working on a treatise analysing the nature of swing and it is hard to get an edge in wordwise.

Saxophonist Emil, the only one of these old friends to stay with music as a profession (trombonist Albert is his younger brother), speaks halting English and Carlo spoke for him as well as himself. Otto, Hans, Emil and Carlo often spoke at the same time. It was difficult to separate their voices when I was transcribing the tape, though Carlo always eventually emerged from the pack.

'We had Belgian and Dutch musicians playing in Frankfurt until 1944. They played their own songs and they played jazz songs. Arne Halphers played "Johnson Rag" and "Pennsylvania 6-5000". As long as there were no loud drum solos they never had trouble. This Reichmusik man, Heinz Baldauf, checked the repertoire, but he did not know any more than the rest of them. You could buy Benny Goodman records until 1938, then somebody must have realized he was Jewish. After that you could buy Artie Shaw records because they did not know his real name was Arshawsky.

'Baldauf was responsible for juvenile delinquents, which kept him so busy he had not much time left for censoring us. The fathers were in the army; the mothers were working and the boys were left alone. You can imagine. Poor Baldauf, he had his hands full, he wanted no trouble. Once he came up to the bandstand and said to me, "We take jazz records away from the people and you stand here and play the same stuff. I don't like it." But he never gave us any serious problems.

'I had trouble with Baldauf once when I played "Harlem" right after "I Got a Girl in Kalamazoo" in the Schumann Cafe. He always addressed me with the familiar "*du*", but I used the formal "*sie*" with him. "Harlem" is close to "Moten Swing" but with another bridge, and it goes to minor. That was something of a code to German musicians. If a guy came along the street whistling "Harlem", you whistled back.

'Baldauf told me, "You can play 'Kalamazoo' if you like, but please, no 'Harlem'. I draw the line there." '

We all sat down around Otto's table and ate *wurst*, mashed potatoes and salad served by Otto's wife Ursula, a writer. We drank Jung wine. We were joined by a young Polish pianist who had departed from Warsaw just in time during the last days of Solidarity and who was living in a small guest house behind Boosenburg. Normally he practises on one of Otto's two grand pianos all day but it was Saturday, I was here and the others had come to speak with me so he only played some Bach for us, and then we all laughed with his impression of Glenn Gould playing the same piece. I preferred the Gould joke to his own version, but he was a pleasant chap, dedicated to music and obviously pleased to be part of our Western jazz party.

Then Otto, his two sons, Emil and I played 'Tea for Two'. The sons smiled continually, though they were clearly uneasy about their ability on bass and drums. But we were all having fun. It is unusual to hear young people play jazz for the fun of it. It is unusual to hear anyone ditto. It was the first time I had jammed for the fun of it in maybe a year.

I have begun to think of this book as a search for Rosebud, that symbol of Charles Foster Kane's happy youth, a search for the days when jazz was young and poor but laughed and sledded.

They talk now about jazz being dead, or dying, as the true spirit dies off with the pioneers. Jazz has been pronounced dead at least once a generation, so we can discount that. But if not quite drowned yet, then it is barely managing to hold one nostril above water. The snow has turned to slush. The laugh meter is broken.

I get these calls from recently arrived young Americans: 'Hi. You don't know me. I'm a tenor player from Houston and I wondered if you could tell me where to blow in Paris.'

'Well, the French don't really like Americans who come and take their gigs.'

'No. I mean just jam.'

'The French don't jam.'

I write on jazz for the *Herald Tribune* and produce concerts for the American Center. I get many such calls from young American jazz musicians who have come here looking for a culture that appreciates their art. I try to be patient with them and explain that nobody jams in Paris.

Young people who play jazz today are even denied a poverty-stricken war-torn youth. Sometimes I invite them over to play a few tunes. Many of them are in their late twenties. Young is not so young any more. They postpone the decision to stop playing jazz, but they can see no living there, not even anybody to jam with, let alone get paid for. Nothing is less welcome than an unknown young jazz musician, even for $20 a night. Perhaps the times are too peaceful. Maybe we need some devils.

'The French don't jam.' That's a good solid anti-French fact. The French do not go out of their way to say, 'Let's have a blow' to foreigners, but it's not really fair. It's the same everywhere in the 'free' world. Where has the fun gone?

Music students jam together in school, but they're getting a degree. Points. There has to be a 'reason' to play these days. 'Play' is work. A gig, building a new band, teaching your child to play the guitar. Fun is, if not incidental, secondary. Today's young jazz players wind up in high-tech, funk, or teaching other young musicians who will have no place to blow either. Such long odds against making a living doing what you love takes the fun out of just doing it.

The only place I know where professional musicians still jam just for laughs is Eastern Europe. Under authoritarian regimes. They are lucky. They have their devils.

'There may only be a vague connection between jazz and freedom for us jazz people,' says the German critic, producer, writer and broadcasting executive Joachim-Ernst Berendt: 'We are much more vague in general than totalitarians. Perhaps we are surprised by our own power. I think people like Goebbels and Stalin knew exactly how strongly jazz implies freedom, and that's why they were so outspoken about suppressing it. Maybe it was only instinctive, but they knew they were being threatened. They knew the power of art, of communication in general, that's why they could move so many millions. They knew that jazz generates the kind of attitude that might shake their power. It can be no accident that totalitarian regimes are all against jazz. It's basic to their character. You improvise, you make your own decisions. You have a special sound, you do not sound like anybody else. Spontaneity means freedom. Bend notes, stretch the rhythm, negate the rhythm if you like. While totalitarian music is martial, right on the beat; you march in step. Goebbels was a master at influencing people and he banned jazz because his instinct told him that listening to jazz was a bad influence on good Nazis.'

Berendt laughed. 'I know Leningrad well. I looked into it from the outside for two years. I made my first radio broadcast during

the siege of 1943. My commanding officer knew I loved swing
music and had a secret collection and he asked me to bring back
some records when I went home on leave. He said, "Swing is good
for morale." So I was playing the same music over the German
army broadcasting service you could go to prison for listening to in
Berlin and Hamburg. And I know for a fact that many of my
listeners were Communists. Totally crazy.'

From the essay 'Red Music' by Czech writer Josef Skvorecky,
now a Canadian resident, who recalls being seventeen and blowing
a saxophone during the occupation:

> There was a band in Prague that called itself Blue Music and we,
> living in the Nazi protectorate of Bohemia and Moravia, had no
> idea that in jazz blue is not a colour, so we called ours Red. But if
> the name itself had no political connotations, our sweet, wild
> music did; for jazz was a sharp thorn in the sides of the power-
> hungry men, from Hitler to Brezhnev, who successively ruled in
> my native land.
>
> Totalitarian ideologists loathe art, the product of a yearning
> for life, because they cannot control it. So art becomes protest
> like it or not. Popular mass art, like jazz, becomes mass protest.
> That is why the ideological guns and sometimes even the police
> guns of all dictatorships are aimed at the men with the horns.

The 1984 Novosibirsk jazz festival consisted of five concerts in
four halls with forty musicians from six Soviet cities. Czechoslovakia's 'first lady of jazz', the singer Jana Koubkova, produced a
forty-minute programme titled 'Women in Jazz' for Czech TV's 'Jazz
Podium' series in 1983. The same year, Hungarian TV presented a
series of highlights of four jazz concerts in Budapest.

These items were culled from the pages of *Jazz Forum*, published
bi-monthly in Polish and English in Warsaw, 'the only international
jazz magazine'. A report from the Republic of South Africa ('Black
bassist Johnny Dyani pays a tribute to his fellow, white, expatriate
Harry Miller, who died in a road accident in Holland') is placed
alphabetically between Poland ('Lodz Jazz Festival: small is beautiful') and Romania ('Although the rain poured, it failed to dampen
the youthful enthusiasm of the third annual jazz festival in
Costesti').

'We are more like a family than a commercial enterprise, ' says

editor Pawel Brodowski. 'The names and addresses of our corres-
pondents in thirty countries are listed in every issue. If you want to
find out about jazz in London, Budapest, Bombay, Christchurch or
Paris, just write. They will be happy to answer. They know each
other and get together often at festivals and meetings. We bring
the world of jazz together.'

Red Mitchell, the bassist, says that there are two sides to our
nature: we are both individuals and group animals. The world is
divided into two major 'isms'. One says 'me-first', the other 'group-
first'. We are told we must choose. But why? Why deny one side of
our nature? Why can't we be both individual and group animals at
the same time? He lives in Sweden because it comes closest to
allowing the two sides to exist. A jazz band is a perfect model to
illustrate the two sides. You can hear three notes from Zoot Sims
and know it's Zoot. At the same time he's kicking the rhythm
section. It equals more than the sum of four people. Jazz unites
people, it can help bring the world together.

We are living in a world where palaces are more important than
sleds. Numbers come before notes. Numbers are never far under
the surface with 'me-first' George Benson, whom I interviewed
shortly after my Boosenburg weekend: 'I'm part of history. *Breezin'*
is the best-selling jazz album of all time.'

Benson was wearing a charcoal pinstripe suit which fit like
another layer of skin. Lounging in his penthouse suite overlooking
Knightsbridge, he would appear homeless without luxury. 'This
Masquerade', the only vocal cut from Grammy-winning *Breezin'*,
became the first song in history to hold the number-one spot on
jazz, pop and soul charts. 'It's a classic.' More facts. Numbers make
jazz history today. 'Hey, Joseph,' he called his valet. 'Did you put
that champagne in the refrigerator?'

Miles Davis once called Benson, 'the baddest guitar player in the
world', and Benson 'knew he wasn't just jiving me'. But being 'bad'
wasn't enough. Benson is a product of his culture, and today's
culture equates money and what it buys with psychic worth.
'When I started out,' he says, 'the greatest jazz musicians in the
world were only making $2,500 a week.' (His mentor, Wes

Montgomery, however, achieved his dream: to own a pair of alligator shoes and a white Cadillac.) Once Benson began to consider $2,500 'only', there was no turning back. He changed producers like shoes, planned hits like advertising campaigns, learned how to sell songs and himself. When he was accused of being a 'traitor to jazz', he responded: 'My job is to make other people happy. I'm an entertainer. I don't remember signing any vows in church to be faithful to jazz.'

The entertainer was obviously, if not embarrassed, defensive. After having entertained 6,000 people, he spoke to the young members of Art Blakey's Jazz Messengers whom he had invited backstage on their night off from Ronnie Scott's club. He rapped with them about the old days on the road, about Wes and Miles and Trane and the others he had blown with. He was once one of the cats himself, a member of that admittedly snobbish fraternity he had resigned from when he started to sing and sell songs. Becoming a 'part of history' involves automatic isolation. He was trying perhaps a bit too hard to be brotherly as the young brothers looked at him with a mixture of respect and doubt. Would they be earning 'only' $2,500 a week when they were his age? Or would they too one day be standing between their chauffeur, valet and a journalist, a white raincoat draped over their shoulders like Italian royalty?

The Crusaders, another band I interviewed around the same time, are a group of intelligent jazz musicians who have become rich and famous by playing music which is beneath their intelligence. They define the contemporary perspective out of which we are looking back. Saxophonist Wilton Felder: 'It's hard for young people who play jazz today to find others in their age bracket to play with. These days kids who play music tend to dye their hair purple and find some gimmick to get rich quick.'

The members of the Crusaders grew up together jamming in Houston; they have worked together for twenty-six years. Keyboardist Joe Sample picked up Felder's train of thought with a six-second break, like between two tracks on an LP: 'A lot of them stop there. Playing jazz is hard. It takes years of muscle-building and mental training. These guys say, "Hey, I make a lot of money. Why break my neck to learn more?" But their mistake is the fact

■ 'Here I am in uniform with a Gypsy, four Negroes and a Jew.' Dietrich Schulz-Koehn with Django in front of La Cigale

■ Ghetto Swingers emblem

■ Dietrich Shulz-Koehn's illegal jazz letter

■ POW letter of thanks for records and needles

■ Double page from camp song book

■Ghetto Swingers, directed by Martin Roman. Fritz Weiss is second
from the left

■Close-up of Fritz Weiss from the propaganda film

■Belgian band at Stalag VI J, 1943

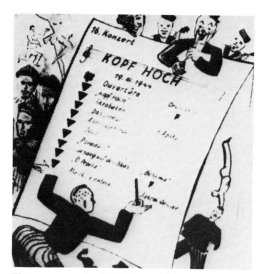

■ Programme for 1944 German jazz concert

■Cinema at Buchenwald

■Record label with its Stalag control stamp

■Publicity photo of Herb Flemming, sent by him with 'sincere personal regards, to a member of Berlin's swing gang', 1936

■Jack Hylton

■Arne Halphers Orchestra, with Greta Wassberg, vocals, 1936

■Jack Hylton Orchestra programme, Scala, February 1937

■Ernst Van't Hoff's orchestra, 1940

JEAN OMER

■Henry Hall publicity shot, Scala, February 1939

■Publicity photo of Jean Omer, sent by him to Hans Bluthner *'en toute "Swing"',* 1942

■Armstrong being made a member of the Hot Club of Berlin, 1952. Hans Bluthner is on the left

■Dietrich Schulz-Koehn, Magdeberg, 1939

Satchmo

Filaming Hotel
Las Vegas nevada.
U.S.A.
Dec, 9th, 1950

Dear Hans"
I received your wonderful letter and as ever glad to get it. I am sending to you, a picture of me. you Called back, a lot of the good old Memories when you sent me the list of my Recordings some of them, I had almost forgotten. Give My regards to all of the Hot Club Members. I have told quite a few Trumpet Players to write you a letter Concerning the ANSATZ-CREME. Maybe you Can help them And any time you should have some more Creme on hand, and wish to send it to Me, Just send in Care of Hugues Panassie, in FRANCE — in Care of my Manager, Mr. Joe Glaser. C.O.D. MANAGER # 745. FIFTH AVE-NEW YORK U.S.A. And thanks Pal, in advance. Will write again soon. Yours for ever, a Friend,
Louis Armstrong

■Letter from Louis Armstrong to Hans Bluthner, December 1950

■Lester Young with Hans Bluthner, Berlin, 1953

that styles change in five years – hell, five *months* – and then somebody else comes up and they're finished.'

The drummer Ndugu Chancler looked straight ahead, thinking hard, and spoke with intense grammatical and rhythmic precision: 'Today's scene defies the basic laws of music. It's like a gold rush. Even if a kid practises hard and interests himself in all sorts of musical facets, the people he plays with most likely won't know anything at all. He's frustrated. He says, "I better forget what I know and do what everybody else is doing." So he dyes his hair purple too. Musical standards are so low right now that it's embarrassing to experienced players like us who have spent half our lifetime learning our craft. We have this whole bank of knowledge, technique, feeling and integrity, and we have to sacrifice it all to stay in the mainstream.'

So jamming on a Saturday afternoon with Otto Jung and the others in Boosenburg was a time-machine back to the days when jazz was fun, when we slid on sleighs and laughed in the snow, when jazz musicians *were* the mainstream and money had nothing to do with it. Playing 'Tea for Two', perhaps we did not sound as tight as the Crusaders, but we were not defying any basic laws either. However, we could afford to have fun. Except for Emil, who is established and gets steady work, we all make our living doing something else.

Carlo Bohlander is too thin and weak to blow a trumpet, though he can talk up a storm. He talked as we played. Otto looked at him: 'Please?!' When we put our instruments down, he fought through the flurry of voices again and most of this story is Carlo's.

The Frankfurt Hot Club was formally organized in 1941. It was summertime. The livin' was not easy. The Battle of Britain was raging. Hitler and Stalin, having digested eastern Europe, were digesting each other. In France, the bread ration had just gone down from 350 to 275 grammes a day; meat from 360 to 250 a week. The freight trains of Europe were packed with chimney fodder.

In Frankfurt, young 'monkeys' jammed in the back room of Horst Lippman's restaurant. A guard in front would ring back by phone if the Gestapo appeared and everybody dashed through the security exit. When Carlo got a job playing rickety-tick music with older men, Hot Club members followed him there to sit in. The orchestra was happy to sit out for a few beers. Soon there were daily jam sessions. Swing brought in customers, so the management did not object. By coincidence, the regular band would always be playing when the Gestapo arrived.

Otto: 'We had long hair.'

Emil: 'Dressed English-style.'

Carlo: 'Wide pants.'

Otto: 'To look as different from the military as possible. The SS man Baldauf ordered Emil to the hairdresser a few times. Emil was a teenager, he is younger than the rest of us. He was controlled more often.'

In 1983, German TV ran a show about the Hot Club and invited the surviving members – Otto, Emil and Carlo included – to talk about it. Carlo mentioned Baldauf, and three days later Baldauf called Carlo. They had not spoken to each other in almost forty years.

'I may have been hard but I wasn't inhuman,' Baldauf said. 'You should be kind to me.'

Testifying in Baldauf's de-Nazification trial, Carlo could say nothing against him. It was common knowledge that their friend Gerd Pick was half-Jewish and Baldauf had never taken action against him. He never once questioned Carlo about why he was not in the army. Carlo played jazz; Baldauf knew it. Carlo figures: 'He must have liked the music or he would have done something to stop it. I am convinced that if another Gestapo man had been in his place, the jazz situation in Frankfurt during the war would have taken a change for the worse.'

Otto remembered Carlo jamming in uniform: 'It was the first time we met: November 1941, remember? We cut a record. I still have it.' Carlo was discharged from the army in November 1942, with the help of a '*Guten-Tag*' doctor. *Guten-Tag* doctors greeted new patients with '*Guten-Tag*' instead of '*Heil* Hitler'.

Louis Freichel was wounded in the hand on the Russian front. He wore a glove and told the doctors it was paralysed. The hand did not move when the doctors tested it with electric shocks. Freichel was sent home, where he immediately took off the glove and played 'Ain't Misbehavin' ' on the piano.

Carlo Bohlander left his harmonium with a friend who had a Jewish mother and an Aryan father: 'The father died of natural causes. Then they sent the mother to the concentration camps.

She died there. The harmonium was confiscated along with everything else. Remember the Milt Herth trio in the thirties? Herth played harmonium.'

Otto: 'O'Neil Spencer was the drummer.'

Hans: 'The Lion Smith on piano.'

Carlo: 'The Lion Smith? Are you sure? Oh, it's probably so. Hans knows these things. My mother had to go and get the harmonium out. They asked, "What does your son do?" She said, "He's in the army." They checked with Baldauf and he said I was OK. You see, I never suffered from that SS man.'

This story where one mother gets taken away to the camps and the other mother gets her son's harmonium back so that he can say he never suffered from this nice SS man is for the birds. I'm out to lunch.

To be fair, I must add this bit of misfiled transcript: 'People did not actually believe . . .' Carlo hesitated. 'No normal mother would believe that you could put people into stoves, you know. It couldn't be true, people cannot conceive of such monstrosities.' Then he laughed and pointed to Emil. 'But Emil was just a juvenile delinquent. He liked to make trouble.'

Emil (haltingly): 'We go in the streetcars . . . pull the . . . emergency cord . . . it stops and it is dark in the car . . . could not . . . prank.'

Otto: 'This was not a consciously political act. But during the Nazi time all these things we did were against authority in general, like the punks now.'

Carlo: 'I understand what Emil was doing and thinking, but there was no real resistance against the Nazis. People consented to it in their hearts somewhere.'

Otto: 'Generally the German people were for the Nazis. They turned against them only when they began to fail.'

Emil: 'Our friends did not want to go into the Hitler Youth, I believe there was resistance to the Hitler Youth.'

Otto: 'There was order. The Germans like order.'

Carlo (ironically): 'The trains ran on time.'

The sun sets over the Rhine.

Carlo (reading a letter from a certain Herr Axmann to Heinrich Himmler): ' "This Anglophile swing youth . . . their activities in the

Fatherland could do damage to the German folk tradition . . . they should be sent to camps, made to work . . ." '

Himmler sent Reinhard Heydrich, who was in charge of Czechoslovakia (and about to be assassinated), the Axmann report, with a covering letter: 'I think these children should be radically exterminated.'

Carlo (shakes his head and taps his temple): 'That was the Nazis, no half measures. "Radically exterminated". Do it right, go all the way.' (Reads the letter again): ' "All young people of that style, male or female, and all teachers or parents who support them, should be sent to concentration camps. They should be whipped." '

Otto switched to bass because pianos were broken down all over Europe, dead as the tuners. Otto and Carlo worked together in the mess hall of an army barracks. They played waltzes and marches and German folk music and jazz in between. Carlo welcomed 1944 with 'Auld Lang Syne' at exactly midnight on New Year's Eve. It is a Scottish song, but nobody noticed.

Otto: 'Remember, they loved it when we improvised.'

Carlo: 'All people react to syncopation.'

Emil: 'Those were nice times. We were all together.'

Carlo: 'They were not nice times. They were very bad times. I do not want any part of them back. One thing is important, though: when you fight for something, there's a spirit. It's a feeling of accomplishment. I came from the right circles. My parents were good average citizens, not particularly nationalist. But when I discovered "Smoke Gets in Your Eyes", I thought . . . I am neither Jewish nor Negro, I am born and raised here from a centuries-old Frankfurt family. Everybody calls this music strange. Maybe I am strange if I like it. But then I discovered others who liked it and they were strange like me.

'I never cared in my life about race, this is the point I want to make. I bet there are more black people who swing, but you also have black ones who don't swing and whites who swing like hell. I don't care, I don't give a damn about it. I can even be proud to be part of the Germany that produced Goethe.

'I can be proud of Ernst Hollerhagen even though he was German. He was the best of all – Ernst Hollerhagen, born in Wuppertal. Before the war he took Swiss citizenship. This man was good enough to play in the States but he was not recognized here at home. Because he was not black, he was German. I think this is one reason why, later, after the war, he committed suicide. He knew he was the best, he played clarinet as good as Benny Goodman, but he had not been born black or Jewish or American.

'In 1942 Ernst Hollerhagen was playing in Frankfurt with Teddy Stauffer and the Teddies. He walked up to his musician friends who were sitting at a table in the Schumann Cafe, he clicked his heels, raised his right arm, and said in a loud voice so everyone could hear: *"Heil* Benny!"'

6
Ruins, Arrests, Martial Law, Fear, Uprisings, Assassination, Occupation and Death

This is my third Warsaw Jazz Jamboree. I am always happy to come, but once I arrive I always wonder why. Perhaps it is my Slavic (Russian) ancestry. It may be masochism, a fascination with suffering, my own and the suffering of others. I am always happy to leave.

Jazz is still in the trenches in Poland. This is the 'Golden Age' of Eastern jazz, fools' gold.

I am sitting in one of those restaurants in peace-torn Warsaw where anybody with a shopping-bag full of zlotys or one two-dollar bill can eat like a king, the king's valet anyway. Josef Balcerak, across the table, has dragged himself more than limped through the door and he seems to be wasting away before my very eyes.

I have lost six kilos in the past year and I imagine myself resembling Balcerak next year. Neither of us may be alive to read this book. Balcerak's own prediction: 'I will not be alive to read your book.'

Josef Balcerak moved with the Soviet army from Warsaw to Berlin as a war correspondent. Everybody was collecting spoils. He liberated a gramophone from an abandoned death room. He began liberating records, variety and symphonic music, from the ruins. In a town in East Pomerania he happened upon a collection labelled 'Horst Wessel *Lied*' and such Nazi standards. He was about to step on them when somehow the labels struck him as odd.

He tore them off and found the original labels underneath – Benny Goodman, Coleman Hawkins and Sidney Bechet. He kissed them. Every time the army moved on he packed the gramophone and the records with 'as much care as if they were ammunition'.

A well-known and respected journalist now retired, editor of the magazine *Jazz* after the war, Balcerak has prepared a list of writers, historians and musicians to interview. One of them has written thirty books on the Polish resistance. He was arrested the first day of martial law, 13 December 1982. Hard to keep track of martial laws in this country. He does not answer his phone.

There is a musician who played jazz in ghetto cafes during the occupation; he hid out and took part in the Warsaw uprising, but he is dead. Hard to keep track of uprisings, occupations and death.

Sipping tea, Balcerak says: 'We have in Warsaw during the war a few assassinations. For instance chief of police of Gestapo was shot not far from this restaurant. One musician was in busy cafe when group of underground men shot few Gestapo. This may also be part of your subject.'

Ruins, arrests, martial law, fear, uprisings, assassination, occupation and death – our subjects. I remembered Claude Verses' question: 'Why do you want to do this book?' I have an answer. Survival. To learn about survival. I am not surviving and must know why and learn how.

Balcerak sends me to the Jewish Historical Institute, a dusty, cold series of offices with broken men poring over old books, handwriting letters on cracked paper, sipping tea from glasses. Stone-cold Kafka, this place stinks ghetto. (A US embassy employee said, 'It's hard to have sympathy for the Poles, they are such fucking racists.') Marion Fuchs is a musicologist who survived the ghetto, published articles about musicians and music in the ghetto, all kinds of music; he knows this subject. But a bent man over a dusty desk indicates with sign language that Fuchs is sick and nobody else speaks either English or French.

One witness is in the hospital; his wife sounds helpful but not hopeful. 'He is sick, he will not be better before the end of the festival.' Sickness is also our subject.

Another witness died last year.

On the afternoon of the last day of the festival, Josef Balcerak calls my hotel room to suggest: 'You know, you must find out about George Scott, a black man who played jazz during the occupation.'

George Scott was called George on stage only. Friends called him Jurek, diminutive of Jerzy. He lived in the centre of town, 16 Widok Street.

He lived in a modest flat on the first floor which he shared with his mother and a sister, Dezzie, Daisy, who was a dancer. They had a radio. Being a stateless person with an international Nansen passport, he had that right. Poles were not allowed to have radios. Polish friends of his came to his house to listen to the news from London.

During the war he played in the Cafe Bodega for Poles, but also for Germans in the Savoy. Polish restaurants and cafes closed before curfew; Germans continued until late at night. He was very popular. His unusual personality created a special atmosphere people liked. His natural charm and good looks attracted women.

Eugeniusz Mossakowski, bassist: 'I don't know what you are going to do with this information but, if there is a single word against George Scott, do not put my name under it. I cannot say anything bad about this man.

'No, I never worked in his band, but he was a good friend of mine. He was an honest fellow with a very good heart. There were slanders against him. People claimed to have seen him sitting on a German tank during the Warsaw uprising with his accordion calling on the Poles to surrender. But this was a lie. I was also taken prisoner by the Nazis and they wanted me to do such thing but I refused and I still survive.

'People were curious and suspicious about how Scott, a creole, managed to live and work legally in Warsaw during the occupation. I can tell you how. His so-called Nansen passport protected him.

'He had a Polish mother and a Negro father. His mother was a circus actress. He was brought up in Poland, he could speak Polish without an accent. He wore a bushy black moustache, combed his hair up and a bit to the side, he was very handsome and always elegantly dressed.

'Scott was extremely talented. He started to play xylophone as a child, then he learned to play drums and accordion. He played with Henry Gold in Cafe Club. George was one of the first "Hotters", as they used to call the musicians who could improvise. He was the first to improvise on the accordion. When he played the drums, his tongue hung out and he played with total energy, he sweated like he was in a sauna bath.

'He had an excellent band when he was performing in the Swan in the Italian Passage, Warsaw. The last time I saw him was in the winter of 1945; we went together from Kraków to Zakopane to play in a restaurant on the top of Gubalowska Hill. The cable railway had been destroyed by the withdrawing Nazis, so we climbed up the hill carrying our instruments.

'On 13 February I got married in Kraków. Soon after that Scott, persecuted by slanderers, decided to leave Poland.'

Edmund Fetting, actor: 'I became interested in jazz listening to my brother, who was seven years older than me and who could play the piano. Many of his jazzman friends visited our house. I used to listen to them and soon I learned to play the piano without reading notes. It was a close shave; I could have been a jazzman but it turned out I became an actor.

'When the Nazis occupied Warsaw I was attending grammar school. I was so fascinated by jazz that I used to sneak out at night and go to the Cafe Bodega, between Chmielna and Nowy Swiat Streets, to hear George Scott.

'At the beginning they looked on me as a curiosity in the Cafe Bodega. I was less than fifteen and it was a very elegant and expensive restaurant. Soon, however, I made friends with the musicians and the staff and they got used to this odd young guest who just wanted to listen to the music.

'There was a bar with a very nice barmaid. She treated me like she was my mother, always offering me tea and sandwiches free. So I could listen to George Scott and his orchestra without being bothered.

'As I remember him, George Scott was creole, most likely of American origin; the shape of his nose and his tightly curled hair were classically Negro. He put brilliantine on his hair to make it glitter, and powder on his face to keep it dry. But he put so much energy into his show that sooner or later his face would be covered with beads of sweat. He would rub it with snow-white handkerchiefs, leaving orange powder smudges on them, which always made me laugh.

'Scott was a dandy, always elegant in smart suits, sometimes dinner jackets, and he used to change his white shirts in each intermission because they were wet with perspiration. He had very good manners.

'He led a big band in Bodega with some of the best young musicians in Warsaw. I don't know where they are now. It is difficult to say now whether Scott was an excellent musician or whether it was his complexion that made him the number-one attraction in Warsaw. Anyway for me as a teenager he was absolutely marvellous, and I never heard anybody say the contrary. The colour of his skin, sparkling eyes, white shirts and his dynamic stage personality certainly attracted women. He had a lot of charm, he flirted all the time. But he never overdid it. It was all perfectly natural for him.

'The place was always packed. Naturally some people came to Bodega just to drink vodka and couldn't care less for the music, but the majority listened when the George Scott orchestra played. Apart from being the leader, he was the drummer. He was really showy, doing acrobatic tricks with the sticks and so on. He also had a good command of the piano. I don't actually remember him playing the piano but you could guess he was a master by his skill on accordion. He always had an accordion next to the conductor's podium. It was a Wurlitzer or a Hohner – a very elaborate and complicated model, a real oddity; he could make miracles with it, which thrilled the audience.

'But the highlight of the programme was when he played the drums. Usually this happened during the last piece of the first set and sometimes the second set too. The audience grew absolutely frenetic when Scott played his drum solos. All the spotlights were on him. It was all carefully orchestrated, visually as well as the music.

'The Scott orchestra was a real curiosity. Imagine! A creole musician leading a jazz band in the centre of the city in the middle of the turmoil of war. Some of the customers were uniformed Nazi officers. I do not wish to imply that Scott was a collaborator. I never heard anybody even suspect him of that. In my opinion, the Nazis considered him a harmless crazy person, but at the same time indirectly useful to them. He was one of the few personalities in town who could be counted on to bring together large numbers of people, and this enabled the Germans to keep tabs on certain circles, and when necessary to arrest them right at their table.

'I saw this happen myself at the Cafe Bodega. In such cases, a Nazi patrol would enter the restaurant, the orchestra would stop playing, people would stop talking. Everybody would become tense and watch the Germans. Whenever a rumour spread about a patrol arriving, I'd hide in the musicians' dressing-room. Somehow the Germans never searched backstage. That probably saved my life. After such an incursion the restaurant was half-empty for a week or two but sooner or later everything was back to normal. George Scott was playing there, and this was stronger than fear.

'I left the cafe late and the only trams still running were number 'O' – only for Germans. I rode these forbidden carriages without much reflection. They probably thought I was some official's son. Anyway, I was never bothered, and it was worth the risk to be able to stay until the very end of the concert.

'The George Scott orchestra played from notes. They had scores; I don't know where they got them. There must have been some sort of channel. But they had quite an extended repertoire. One thing I remember: there was a bookshop on Nowy Swiat Street where I used to go to browse often. Sometimes I'd find pictures that would interest me, and once I discovered a Duke Ellington album with "Sophisticated Lady" and "Caravan" and a lot of other numbers. All written for solo piano. The bookseller employed an old man who could sightread piano arrangements note for note. He used to play the Ellington pieces for me and my friends. He had no feeling for syncopation but he could play the melodies. It was there in that bookshop that I learned about Duke's music, then I went home and tried to play it the jazz way.'

Stefan Kisielewski's preface to *Citizen Jazz* by Jerzy Radlinsky Kisielewski, published in Warsaw, 1965:

During the occupation I was taught to play jazz by my room-mate Marek Cybulski, a cafe pianist who had absolutely no technique. But he had this inborn instinct for chromatic harmonies and syncopation. I could leave him behind with conservatory music but with jazz I was a complete idiot. He took his revenge on me in the Rio Rita, a cafe on Krakówskie Przedmiescie Street, where I too worked after a while.

Usually the place was empty but from time to time a group of youngsters who were well-known to the owners would come in. They took advantage of the absence of Germans to request jazz. I'd play 'The Man I Love', 'Stormy Weather' and 'Tea for Two'.

Then somehow I got hold of a beautiful album of Duke Ellington, edited by the master himself. There were piano arrangements of 'Caravan', 'Solitude' and 'Sophisticated Lady'. Later on, being in urgent need of money, I sold this album to a notorious Warsaw bookseller on Nowy Swiat Street who scowled upon it and took it reluctantly. Then the same day he resold it to a friend of mine for four times as much money. I nearly had a stroke.

Edmund Fetting: 'I was collecting and exchanging records throughout the occupation. I managed to assemble quite a collection. I had one rarity, a 78 r.p.m. record of a Count Basie record which I got from my friend Zbyszek Stepowski, a young pianist. But most of my occupation collection was comprised of German Telefunken records. Do you know for example Helmut Zacharias? Now he plays what I call 'money music' but he used to play jazz then, good jazz. There was an American tenor-saxophone player named Tex Beneke. God knows how I remember his name, on Telefunken Records. I had a Nat Gonella record, Earl Hines, Jimmie Lunceford – whatever I could afford.

'I had an excellent record player, but listening at home was not enough for me. During the occupation a Polish profiteer had an ice rink on Pulawska Street with music played through loudspeakers. I made friends with the manager and whenever I came with new records he let me play them over his system. This way he had a constant supply of free new music and I had the pleasure of listening to my beloved records ten times louder. As the people skated joyfully around in circles, I stood right next to the speaker with my legs cramped from the cold and hands frozen stiff but happy and proud that my beloved jazz was resounding all over the street.

Meanwhile, back at the Jamboree . . .

Jazz Jamboree is not like the other festivals. There are so many social, cultural and political levels that it is a privilege just being there, a scoop. Like a sudden truce in a war when the soldiers all of a sudden exchange cigarettes and whisky instead of projectiles. A right time and place. A hole in the wall. A well in the desert. A situation where time is still swing not money. Mankind United (a rugby club).

Opening night, musicians from Poland, West Germany, Britain, Canada, Norway and the USA – many sponsored by their countries' cultural establishments – proved that jazz is one area of international co-operation which functions even in times of political strife. Running an officially sanctioned major jazz festival is a way to give the Russians the finger without risking anything. Swing still has this symbolism in Eastern Europe, and jazz has a broader if not larger appeal than rock. Jazz bridges generational and class gaps with its unique combination of intellectual and physical, avant-garde and commercial and old and new elements. 'Anybody who likes jazz cannot be a Communist,' says one Polish Jazz Society official.

A bemedalled general explaining to the population on prime-time TV why he was not responsible for kidnapping the good Solidarity priest Jerzy Popieluszko even though the kidnappers worked for him is followed directly by Ray Charles live from Congress Hall.

Stability is not the first word that comes to mind describing Poland. Neither is gaiety. And you can't even call it liberal. Ronald Reagan would win in a walk running in Poland. I never once heard a word of Russian, or saw one Russian newspaper. There are also some notable absentees. Except for an East German duo and one lonely Soviet pianist who kept wandering around the hotel lobby buying postcards, no other Eastern-bloc countries were represented. In the past the place was flooded with Czechs and the rest. One Pole smiles with pride: 'They are afraid we will contaminate them.'

No serious Polish note-taking would be complete without a Jaruzelski joke. Jaruzelski decides to join the church instead of fighting it. He starts to pray: 'Oh Lord, please help me. I must find a way to deal with Solidarity.' Lo and behold, Solidarity is dealt with. Encouraged, he prays again: 'Oh Lord, please let me be a man. You know what I mean, with a woman. A real man. Just once.' Sure enough, it works. And then he prays: 'Oh Lord, let me walk on water.' He goes to the river and walks out on it. Two guys sitting on the bank eating sausage and drinking vodka watch him. 'Look at that,' one of them points: 'Those stupid motherfuckers can't even swim right.'

'I'll bet he didn't say "motherfucker".'

The Pole who told the joke shakes a forefinger and nods his head into a blur: 'Yes he did, yes he did!'

Polish jazz fans lean towards a sort of hipper-than-thou stance which can be annoying. They are not aware how square they look trying to appear hip. They have, however, discovered at least one outward trapping of hipness – dope. The sweet smell of cannabis floats in Congress Hall, and home-made smack from Polish poppies is on the market. I saw one freak take off in a doorway, another with his nose on his lap in the first row. Together with the habitual vodka consumption, it adds up to some deep highs. Suicide seems somehow less suicidal in Poland. You cannot tell young Poles: 'Stop that. You're ruining your life,' when their lives have already been ruined for them. The toll is evident. No matter how bad it was in the past, you could always say, 'But the people are so nice.' You can no longer say that. Smiles are rare and bitter and aggression is never too far under the surface. They certainly are fans, though there is also that political credit being here – all eight of Jazz Jamboree's principal concerts were sold out immediately when tickets went on sale in July, four months before the event, without advertising, before the festival was even programmed; and they sit for hours and *listen*. More than 30,000 of them.

This is the twenty-sixth Jazz Jamboree. It has been annual except for 1982, when under martial law a smaller affair called Jazz Manoeuvres was presented. At the time a government spokesman commented favourably on the name; he said how wonderful it was that jazz musicians could maintain their sense of humour during hard times.

Now the following information is sensitive, please consider it off-the-record. A travelling package called the Chicago Blues Festival was about to perform during Jazz Manoeuvres when Brezhnev died. Cultural events were cancelled all over Eastern Europe. But an official of the Polish Ministry of Culture asked a Polish Jazz Society official (even good guys are officials in these places): 'The blues. That is sad music, is it not?' Understanding the point immediately, the jazz official shot right back: 'No. Not sad. *Funereal.*' So there were blues for Brezhnev in Warsaw.

Wieslaw Machan, musician: 'There were many excellent musicians with dance-band experience in Warsaw during the occupation, but few of them could improvise. I had to write out their solos. On the other hand there were a few really good jazzmen. Josef Rosolek, for example, a great clarinet, flute and saxophone player. He was involved with the underground. He could speak perfect German, so he took a job with the band in the Europejski Hotel restaurant, which was for Germans only. Working there and wearing a German uniform he could easily gather information for the Polish underground army of the resistance movement with its head-quarters in London. He helped a lot of people to escape from prisons. He was the first in Warsaw to learn about the Nazi plan to invade the USSR, which he reported to the Allies.

'Tumel, a fantastic instrumentalist who could play anything on almost any instrument, worked with Rosolek at the Europejski Hotel restaurant. Once a German officer came in with some music and asked Tumel to play it. Tumel developed it into a number of improvisations and the German was so happy to hear his creation played in such an imaginative way.

'I played with Tumel at the beginning of the occupation in the Niebieski Motyl (Blue Butterfly) theatre. When I walked into the rehearsal I heard a marvellous trumpet solo with a piano accompaniment. My first thought was, "Well, I thought I was supposed to be the pianist here." But when I looked closer I saw Tumel playing trumpet with his right hand and piano with his left. He was a phenomenon. Tumel had a Jewish fiancée who lived in the ghetto. He used to play there quite often. Tumel ended up dead due to vodka. While the war was still on, he drank himself to death.

'Two or three weeks after Tumel, another splendid jazzman did the same. It was a trombone player – Jaraszewski. Tumel died in bed surrounded by bottles. Jaraszewski first smashed his trombone against the wall and then jumped out of the window of his apartment on Aleje Jerozolimskie Street.

'I played for some time with a wonderful improviser on trumpet and accordion, Bronislaw Stasiak. Whenever I mentioned my plan to leave his band, he joked: "If you do that I'll go to the Gestapo and tell them such things about you you'll go to a concentration camp." I finally did end up in one, Flossenburg, but it wasn't his fault. Stasiak had already been sent to Auschwitz.

'I graduated from the Lvov Institute of Technology, specializing in internal-combustion engines. While I was a student I had a jazz group and we played for dances and parties to earn money for our tuition. Then I worked as an engineer in a factory producing undercarriages. After the invasion, I came back to Warsaw with my wife and brother. I had no money and no job. The family apartment in Warsaw was still standing. We found it completely looted, but at least we had a roof over our heads.

'Then I learned that the Germans were looking for such technicians as myself to work for the German war industry. I moved to another place and took my brother's identity. At the very beginning of the war he had been sent to the Matthausen concentration camp. I started to look for a job as a musician.

'It was not easy. I visited cafes and restaurants and finally found a job as solo pianist in a restaurant run by two Polish marathon champions, Janusz Kusocinski and Josef Noji. The job did not last very long. Kusocinski was arrested, Noji soon followed him and the restaurant was closed.

There were three popular bands in Warsaw – the Krolowie Jazzu (Kings of Jazz), featuring Bronislaw Stasiak; the George Scott orchestra; and I played with Mieczyslaw Klecki and the Zlota Siodemka (Golden Seven) – eventually I took over that band.'

Mieczyslaw Klecki, drummer and bandleader, in his *Aural Encyclopaedia of Polish Jazz*:

World War II did not put an end to the dynamic jazz life in Poland. The German ban on dancing turned former dance orchestras into concert bands. This made them play better; people were now listening to them. The circle of musicians shrank. Ady Rosner and Henryk Wars left for the east before the Germans came. Others were taken away by the occupier. The remaining musicians did surprisingly well for a while.

The Bronislaw Stasiak big band performed in the Blue Butterfly theatre, George Scott the mulatto in the Cafe Bodega. There was also a lot of jazz in the ghetto, Bobby Fiddler and Artur Gold on the top of the list. After Stasiak was taken away to Auschwitz, I organized the Golden Seven with members of his former group, with three saxophones, two trumpets, drums and the excellent composer/arranger Wieslaw Machan on piano.

Wieslaw Machan

Wieslaw Machan: 'Klecki was Jewish. At first everything was OK but then somebody started to blackmail him, threatening to denounce him to the Gestapo. He sold all his belongings and went into hiding. He hid in my apartment for a while and then went to Lublin. There somehow he got himself a job playing in an orchestra for the Gestapo. When the Polish army arrived he joined it and by the time he came back to Warsaw he was a captain.

'There were lots of restaurants and clubs in occupied Warsaw, some for Poles others for Germans. I played only for Poles but there were musicians who were forced to play for Nazis for various reasons. The restaurants were obliged to close before curfew but sometimes people with pockets full of money wanted to stay longer. In that case they had to stay until dawn because walking at night without a permit was very dangerous. On the other hand if a patrol found people in a restaurant at night they could easily just shoot everybody without asking any questions.

'In the Alhambra restaurant the doorman had a special button to push when there was trouble and it lit up a little red lamp over my piano. In a flash the customers would be in a closet and the waiters cleared the tables. The musicians covered themselves with their coats and pretended they were sleeping. All that was done hastily in great panic.

'One time three musicians working in a restaurant dared to play "Warszawianka" in public. This is a patriotic song written in 1831 during a national uprising. All three were executed. The Nazis were very sensitive about such acts of disobedience. They did not permit patriotic songs, no Chopin, no Jewish composers. They wanted only German repertoire, and they even supplied us with appropriate scores. We had to submit a list of what we had played every day. Naturally we lied about it, but we could never be sure who was in the audience. So we always played some of the German numbers. Occasionally I smuggled Chopin in by stating the theme of one of his waltzes and then everybody would improvise on it. It was difficult; he wrote a lot in sharp keys, but we managed, and it was good practice because we were forced to learn how to improvise in sharp keys.

'Jazz in Auschwitz? Yes. Bronislaw Stasiak led a jazz band there for a while. I heard that Maciej Dobrzynsky was playing on drums in this band.

'Music saved my life in a concentration camp. In 1944 I landed in Flossenburg which was not so famous as Auschwitz but it was one of the most cruel. They did not even bother to mark people with numbers, extermination went so fast. Nobody stayed alive there very long. Hundreds and hundreds of people went through the chimneys there every day. And when the crematoriums were not efficient enough the Nazis were just burning people in a fire like wood.

'There was an orchestra there. When we first arrived a preliminary selection was made. Lawyers, engineers, teachers – the intelligentsia – were assassinated immediately. A Polish-speaking German asked about musicians. Many people stepped forward; I had not known there were so many musicians. They thought it might save them. But when they were tested, all false musicians were hung on the gallows right away.

'I was accepted as pianist by the bandmaster. Then I noticed Dominik Gorzelniawski, who was a better pianist than me. So I asked the bandmaster to take him and I would switch to violin. He agreed. It was a quasi-symphony orchestra. All day long we carried heavy sacks and in the evening we had to play the William Tell Overture. Edward Ciesielski, an excellent jazz trumpeter but also a cellist, was to play the solo. His tired stiff fingers could hardly move on the neck of the cello. He was within an ace of the gallows.

'Then they started a so-called jazz band. There were six of us. We could get half a loaf of bread, some marmalade and a few cigarettes. It helped us survive. We syncopated and tried to swing and there were some solo improvisations. I played double bass, and I got pretty good. Thanks to music I not only survived the war but I became a professional bass player.'

These days Government spokesman Jerzy Urban often attacks the 'outrageous propaganda' on the 'Voice of America'. (He often has a point.) But on the day before Jazz Jamboree 1984, VOA disc jockey Willis Conover was welcomed at Warsaw airport by three video crews and a Polish hot band playing 'Take the "A" Train'. Conover's programme 'Music USA' gave a crucial stimulus to Eastern jazz in general and Polish jazz in particular after World War II. 'Williseum Conoverum' is a real hero over here. A father figure, he makes speeches, supporters give him flowers, celebrities go out of their way to have their picture taken with him. He autographs. He has groupies.

'The Poles have a combination of vitality, creativity and sense of humour that is essential to jazz,' he says. 'And it is part of Polish culture to express emotions openly.' Conover's programmes have an estimated 100 million listeners around the world. He has been described by an officer of the United States Information Service as 'one of America's greatest foreign-policy tools'.

In conclusion it should be mentioned that everybody is sure the telephones are tapped, and that hotel rooms are bugged. 'He's KGB/CIA/a Party member.' Take your pick. It doesn't really matter, nobody seems very worried about it. Those stupid motherfuckers can't even swim right.

7

Unblest Historicity

Thirty-five years after the Axis cracked, a Parisian magazine poll voted the Germans the people most admired by the French. Not liked, admired. Italy placed – more liked than admired.

At the end of the *'drôle de guerre'* (weird war) when France surrendered in 1940, the clean, lean, blue-eyed and clear-headed Germans attracted instinctive French collaboration. It was not yet a dirty word. Collaboration implied realistic affirmative action.

In his book *French and Germans, Germans and French*, historian Richard Cobb explores the ambiguity of the word, tainted when Marshal Pétain chose 'the road of collaboration':

> There existed, on both sides, ties of friendship that had been created in the inter-war years; and, finding themselves, almost overnight, in control of the complicated administration of a capital city – an event for which they had never planned ... the Germans sought out in the first place those Frenchmen and Frenchwomen they already knew. A German railway engineer would seek out his opposite number, a German detective would have contacts in the *police judiciare* ...
>
> One of the young (German) university graduates who was all at once to find himself in charge of Paris publishing had written a thesis on a French literary theme and had spent several years as a *lecteur d'Allemand* in the University of Toulouse. He embarked on his new task with a sense of personal excitement, for it offered him a unique opportunity to come into close personal contact – sometimes daily – with all the leading figures of the Parisian literary scene. To see him merely as a censor, the obedient instrument of the Propaganda Staffel, would be to

oversimplify a relationship that was much more personal and
vital. He wanted to get to know as many novelists and poets as
possible, and to publish as many of their works as he could. In
both aims, he was extraordinarily successful; and at the end of
an idyllic four-year stay in the French capital – a city that he
loved – he could look back to a publisher's list of enormous
distinction and variety. His concern throughout had been ... to
see into print the works of a host of authors whom he admired
and liked.

Many sincere French pacifists, veterans of World War I, were
at first grateful to Pétain for having spared their sons a bloody
encore. They rejected Gaullism like American intellectuals reject
'better dead than red'. Some pacifists are accused of cowardice and
the two emotions are often hard to sort out. Thoughtful, church-
going *citoyens* feared decadence and Communism and they
welcomed the National Socialist accent on physical fitness and
the work ethic.

Collaboration – a dangerous word covering this period. On the
other hand it is dangerous to ignore the human element in favour
of the political, to say that any contact between the two parties
involved in an occupation represents a sort of treason on the part
of the occupied. Was a taxi-driver a collaborator when he drove a
German? Was a waiter when he served one? A musician when he
played for one? When music made Germans feel pleasure did this
perhaps make them more reluctant to inflict pain? Is this
collaboration or resistance?

Improvisations on top of the elastic, swinging pulse of jazz
cannot be censored because they exist only in the present. Jazz is
hard to pin down, it appeals to both mind and body. It slips through
the cracks, or at least did before it became a university major.
There was a time when all establishments rejected it; it was
subversive everywhere. Remember, now we are talking not about
the tame dance bands, which were accepted by just about
everyone, but savage exploration by a lone improviser. People who
reveal themselves in public. Naked. These people stand for
everything establishments are against. It can be argued that bebop
lost its power and relevance when Jimmy Carter sang 'Salt Peanuts'
with Dizzy Gillespie, and there would have been no 'Golden Age'
had Joseph Goebbels sung 'St Louis Blues'.

The French smell of armpit, black tobacco and garlic, they while away time in cafes and making love – or at least there are those stereotypes to deal with. As the Gallic boozer turned into the Gallic loser, collaborators wanted to prove they could be bright-eyed and bushy-tailed and keep noses to grindstones. Where neatness counts, order seemed to prevail.

The French would like to be blonde and clean and efficient like the Germans and enjoy life as much as the Italians at the same time. The trains run as scheduled and yet they are forever screaming at each other. Conflicting traditional traits side by side, aggravated by economic fear in the eighties, divide the people. The north vacations in the south to escape its Germanic character as much as to rest. August is a fix, a nationwide nod. The entire country has its nose not to the grindstone but on the table.

Today is 15 August, a holiday that falls on Wednesday this year. So there are '*ponts*', long weekend bridges, on either side of it. If the French spent as much energy and ingenuity working as they do building bridges to avoid it, it might not take more than ten francs to buy a dollar at the moment. The French can spot a span months away. Two adjacent bridges in the middle of a nationwide nod support a spectacular ten-day suspension.

France and Robbie, my little French family, are in Falaise, a hamlet on a southern hillside near Toulon. I'm in a *chambre de bonne* trying to write around midnight. During the day it has befallen me to supervise the working persons who are constructing loft space France and I purchased and hope to move into two weeks from now. These particular working persons kept off the bridges because they are illegal immigrants and political refugees from Chad and Algeria who risk identity checks when they move around (brown skin precludes the need for yellow stars) and anyway they cannot afford the tolls.

During the day I push to make sure the work will be completed before the start of Robbie's school year. They are honest workers who really need no pushing and never complain about their work. They like working for a writer; we have lunch together. We boycott the neat cheap little restaurant across the street since sensing static from *la patronne*, they are sure, due to their brown skin, though the apartment is in a racially mixed neighbourhood.

Having heard his (Jewish) aunt complain about too many Arabs, Robbie grumbled: 'There will be nothing but Arab kids in my new school.' I reminded him that his two best friends in the old school, where he was happy and got good grades, were black and Arab, something he had not even been aware of in the particular. Robbie requires debriefing after each visit with his aunt and uncle, kind childless people who love him very much and who would certainly deny racist tendencies.

Writing at night in the quiet, empty city can be lonely and I look forward to calling France after eleven, when the rates go down.

Tonight at eight, however, I met Claude Verses in a fancy restaurant where Gene Guitar was working. I thought I'd be back too late to call France tonight but Gene Guitar did not work after all. The *maître d'*, a gay German fop who wears grey flannel suits and wide ties, told Verses that their image depended on the 'right clientele' (Prince Rainier of Monaco dined there last week) and wouldn't he be more comfortable in the Mexican restaurant down the street?

A tough rocker *à la* Keith Richard, Gene threw his guitar at the gay German, missing him by inches. Another jazzman throws an axe. Being an outlaw takes its toll.

Guitar and Verses went to snort up their sorrows in a gramme of coke and I came back here to write. Verses generally writes at night too, he felt guilty watching me leave: 'I do the coke,' he grumbled, 'and you get the energy.'

Cocaine is feminine, they call it 'Girl'. Heroin is 'Boy'. Some cynics believe that governments allow Boy and Girl into ghettos to keep the unemployed uncomplaining. They also accuse the entertainment business of stringing out musicians and actors so that they must make commercial albums and movies to pay their dealers. These people probably exaggerate, though facts remain.

In *Doctor Faustus*, Thomas Mann writes:

Our time itself, secretly – or rather anything but secretly; indeed, quite consciously, with a strange complacent consciousness, which makes one doubt the genuineness and simplicity of life itself and which may perhaps evoke an entirely false, unblest historicity – it tends, I say, to return to those earlier epochs; it enthusiastically re-enacts symbolic deeds of sinister significance, deeds that strike in the face the spirit of the modern age, such, for instance, as the burning of the books and other things of which I prefer not to speak.

I prefer not to speak of them myself. But I am dealing here with deeds of great 'sinister significance' and I cannot manage to keep the symbolism in the past.

My publisher has expressed the reservation that this chapter has nothing to do with the subject. 'Facts!' he exclaimed. 'Stick to the facts. Stop contemplating your navel.'

As a matter of fact I have been contemplating my navel. With horror. It has grown bigger as my stomach shrinks. I have, if anything, too many facts. If all of this stuff has nothing to do with 'the subject', why have I lost nine kilos since I first wrote about, and discovered photographs of, the Ghetto Swingers? Is it coincidence that my thighs have shrunk and my cheeks are sunken and suddenly I have become claustrophobic in the metro?

These deeds that strike our face are not necessarily behind us. We can say 'never again', but for a Zulu in Soweto the holocaust is right now. The Afrikaners have found a subtler final solution, which they justify in biblical terms, but I live in Paris and Paris is not yet burning, so why have the kilos gone?

It occurs to me in the dark of the night that we are being continually impressed by brown, black or grey waves. They frown or smile, straight or gay, past and present, it makes no difference. We are Shanghaied. We are at war.

That is why I like to write late at night, when people of good will outnumber those who operate with that 'strange complacent consciousness'. They tend to be early birds. Not that I'm a night owl. Often I fall asleep reading *Asterix* to Robbie at bedtime. Though then I wake up and work before dawn so I can be part of the majority for a while.

I just received a postcard from Dietrich Schulz-Koehn in Liblar, with the sentence: 'Life here goes on and sometimes I feel very lonely and I think what good is it to live or to work?'

Lack of purpose, indecision, a search for some kind of meaning. The world of jazz is clogged with negative emotion. One level removed from direct emotion, we are looking over our shoulders, a negative motion. We think about what we are playing and why rather than just playing. We are obsessed by the size of the audience rather than the quality of the music. What is catching up with us? The synthesizer? Funk? Is 'inefficient' public acoustic interior exploration still functional? Does it reach anybody? Who has time for it? Money to spend on it? Shouldn't we be making more noise? Has 'the classical music of the twentieth century' lost its relevance before that century even ends?

I must consider the possibility that there are youngsters as fiery as Charlie Parker was, and I just don't know about them. But jazz is my game. I talk to people, get around. I don't hear renewal on any but the most exceptional terms, a player here and there. There is no cultural centre; styles blur and overlap – cultural confusion aggravated by economic insecurity. In the larger context, the old political assumptions also blur. Right and left are no longer automatic definitions; we have no place to direct our hate.

This may be one reason South Africa is such a unanimous target, even for those who are racists in their own countries. Afrikaners have a point when they say that too many people living in glass houses are throwing stones, but they have constructed the only system *based* on racism since Nazi Germany. It is the closest thing we have to the devil incarnate; black townships are not all that different *in kind* from concentration camps. And here too, like the banning of jazz in the Third Reich, art is thrown into the centre of the fray with the cultural boycott. It is no accident that so much fine, passionate literature comes out of South Africa, much of it banned, where the written word can be compared to jazz under the Third Reich. The devil provides purpose.

At this late hour I think about Claude Verses, head full of Girl, and, lately, more and more, Boy – chopping, weighing and packing across town. He is aware of . . . obsessed with the fact that dealing drugs as an Afro-American alternative to sweeping up for a living is a cliché. He wrote a poem titled, 'Out of the Garbage Can on to the Mirror'.

Sampling leftovers from the pile, chopper's prerogative, he shuffles stanzas from file to file, trying to avoid thinking about the 'outraged black poet' cliché. With 'A Liberal Cut', another poem, he takes pride in pushing an inferior product, thus adding a poetic level to the 'Jewish ghetto merchant' cliché.

> Revenge is a shady mixture.
> This tawny nostril,

Exhausted flare,
Ingests another fine mess
While the chimney
Spawns white cinders
Which I step on.
Ouch wits.

Stockbrokers and account executives file through his parlour in Montmartre buying Girl so that Verses can afford to file stanzas, occasionally published in obscure Swiss reviews, instead of becoming a working person. He is fascinated by my working persons. 'Massah boss-man, whup them nigger mothers,' he chides me. 'Make 'em shake their black asses.' You could cast Verses as Grumpy in *Snow White*, or Sneezy.

He was living with his German woman, Blow Black's sister-in-law, and her teenage son from a previous liaison. His work table is in their dining-room. He grumbles that the son and his friends plunder his cigarettes and canned cous-cous, listen to Al Jarreau records too loud and forget his phone messages. Customers file through to exchange banknotes for small folded packets while family life goes on around them. Mother and son do not seem aware that the people are customers, and nobody is introduced. But I suspect Verses of playing Smiley with his German woman when nobody's looking.

The price of a bottle of scotch went down fifteen francs last week, a litre of gas went up fifty centimes. The conclusion is obvious: drink more and drive less. I called Verses to tell him about it, hoping to cheer him up after the bad news in the restaurant. I felt like a good German re-enacting a symbolic deed of sinister significance, like cheering up a Jew under the Third Reich.

'"Opposition and superstition,"' he said. '"A victim of scorn." Not bad. Two lines tonight.'

It took eight dials getting through to France. Everybody calls over the bridge after the rates go down. France is big on bad news; bad news provides good conversation. I was anxious to tell her the bad news about Verses, and how excited I was to be writing a book structured to contain that sort of information. But she was faster off the mark. France wins the conversational dash, the marathon too.

Except for two retired Parisian couples, Falaise is deserted in winter. In the summer it is overrun by a working-class family from Toulon – four generations, including third cousins – of regimental proportions. They campaign rather than play. The adults are fat and raucous tailgaters, much more Italian than German, who shoot *boules* on a flat piece of land down behind the village. The children shout and scream, riding bikes and kicking footballs. Their ancestors once farmed the land around the village. The Toulonais family considers Falaise occupied territory. Parisian occupiers make sure to be somewhere else in July and August.

We were house-sitting for one of them. France had been advised not to allow Robbie to play with the redneck, lowbrow children from Toulon. We were paying no rent so she did not argue, but Robbie was soon down there shouting, screaming, riding and playing football with the rest of them. He disappears for hours and comes back with breathless tales of tents, great trees to climb and winning ping-pong games by wide margins.

Robbie does not know the difference between a redneck and a highbrow, but today there had been an argument with one of the cousins. The child cried and went to get her mommy. It was not much of an argument, nobody got hurt, and it was over by the time the woman arrived. She shouted hysterically about being tired of providing Robbie with snacks, and said that anyway the piece of land down behind the village belongs to them (the Parisians say it's *theirs*), and Robbie was no longer welcome.

The story clocked nine minutes. Obviously France had better bad news than me, so I only said: 'This is costing a fortune.'

'You sound depressed.'

'Well, it's a shitty world. The bad news I've been reading, writing, thinking about. What kind of world did we bring Robbie into? It's wiping the smile off his face. So he has nobody to play with tomorrow?'

'You take everything so seriously,' she sighed. 'It'll blow over tomorrow.'

But it won't. Even if it does, it will blow back the day after. It might even blow *up*.

And I don't mean distant places like Ethiopia or Manila. Right next door, Corsicans blow up French policemen, Welsh people set fire to Welsh houses owned by English people, Walloons trash Flemish property, Basques blow up Spanish people, the Irish blow up the Irish, the Irish blow up the English, Palestinians blow up Parisian synagogues, Libyans assassinate Libyans in Paris, and there are French working persons who do not sneeze at a final solution to the Arab working-person problem.

The Falaisians are pleased about the strong showing by the extreme right-wing party of Jean-Marie Le Pen in recent elections. Le Pen's platform is, 'Kick out the foreigners so the French can get back to work.' They're after working people of darker hues, but I'm foreign too. Le Pen received 'only' ten per cent of the vote; intellectual friends say he is no serious threat. Intellectuals said that about Hitler, who wanted the foreigners out so the Germans could get back to work. Do the Falaisians know that Robbie is fifty per cent American and one hundred per cent Jewish?

Well, I don't want to stay where I'm not wanted, but we just bought an apartment in Paris. I make my living here, such as it is; France has a good job. It's not easy to start over somewhere else when you're past fifty. And where? I left New York fifteen years ago.

Anyway, it will all blow over tomorrow.

8
Baldauf

Carlo Bohlander arranged an interview with the ex-SS man Heinz Baldauf and I went back to Frankfurt for it. There was an afternoon – excuse the expression – to kill before our 7p.m. appointment and as Carlo took me for a walk around town, we passed the Park Hotel where Polish author (*Notebook of a Dilettante*) Leopold Tyrmand, now deceased, then vice-president of the Rockford Institute in northern Illinois, worked in 1943 in Frankfurt under a condition called *Zwangsarbeit* – forced labour – waiting on tables. Forty years later he had delivered a speech only a few blocks away, as part of a conference 'On Freedom'.

His speech began:

Freedom, all its mobilizing power notwithstanding, is a notion laden with myriad implications and purports. The longer we live the more we suspect how deviously it can be perverted, and the less we trust the certitudes for which, forty years ago, we were so ready to risk our lives. Let me, therefore, focus on one illustration, motivated as I am by what the Italians call *'intelletto d'amore'*. In 1942, during my first Polish underground briefing in Vilna, now Lithuania, the music blasting out, disguising the meeting as a dance, was Fats Waller's 'Ain't Misbehavin' '; in Oslo, Norway, in 1941, my Hjemmetronten cell's anthem was 'A Tisket A Tasket' . . . Ella Fitzgerald sang words that were pregnant with hope: '. . . and someone help me find my basket and make me happy again . . .' and the entire gathering cheered.

Is there a lesson in it? Does jazz teach us something about freedom – one of the most complex of all the spiritual and social concepts with which Judeo-Christian civilization ever had to struggle? There were some among us, certainly, who pondered the Constitution and the American promise, or dream, but for most of us the collective improvisation of a dixieland combo came to mean, if only subliminally, the perfect emblem of freedom and all the necessary energy to defend it. It was an image of liberty whose dynamics, at the time, seemed invincible, the ultimate representation of free utterance, the typification of a situation where anyone plays his own tune, providing he submits to a wise and superior arrangement.

Jazz was to us a system of latitudes subject to a freely accepted discipline of integral bonds between an individual and a group. As such it became perhaps the best metaphor for liberty that any culture has ever come up with. It conveyed a message that there is a central authority – usually with a trumpet in hand – to which one is responsible for holding the proper key and beat and who is entitled to a proper share of expression – and this is exactly what constitutes the principles from which a genuine order of freedom emerges. It became the quintessential allegory for the pluralism of opportunities within which anyone who knows how to use an instrument and contribute to a common sound can make a statement about what he believes is beautiful and true.

In 1943, in a Frankfurt Wirtschaft on Neue Mainer Strasse, I listened, at a clandestine jam session, to Sidney Bechet's 'Really the Blues'. I sat next to a German of my own age, in uniform but on leave. 'It's my record,' he said proudly. 'I was in a Panzer division in France. When we took a town, the others went after pâté and I looked for the music shops.'

I asked, 'What does this music make you think of?'

'Free people,' he said. 'Don't ask me why.'

Carlo came along as moral support and to translate; Baldauf spoke very little English. I wondered why he had agreed to meet me. Probably has something to sell. We walked one flight down to the Opel Stube, a restaurant in an industrial wasteland underneath an automobile sales agency. It was empty except for an overweight barman. We took a table in the corner.

'You are nervous?' Carlo asked me.

'I never met a Gestapo officer before.'

'Think of it this way,' he laughed. 'He was just a police detective.'

'That's why I'm nervous.'

It was Baldauf who had suggested the Opel Stube, which was near his house. There was something ominous about the place, reminding me of the old war-movie line, 'I don't like it, Joe, it's too quiet.' Obviously something went on here; this was some sort of hangout for some kind of people at some other time and I wasn't sure I wanted to know who.

Baldauf came in, shook hands and ordered a brandy with a beer chaser. I ordered a schnapps ditto. He was seventy, looked younger, of medium height with a full head of grey hair with black eyebrows. Wearing a sombre suit, white shirt and blue tie, he looked like the man in the street. You would not look twice at him on a West German street.

He pulled out an envelope bulging with photocopies of official documents, character references from his war-crimes trial in Nürnberg. . .

An official declaration signed Herr Horst Lippman, 49 Kaiser-strasse, Frankfurt, dated 12 February 1947:

In 1944 the Gestapo accused me of listening to foreign radio stations and making propaganda with English and American jazz music. Mr Baldauf testified, but he was always correct and proper with me and showed understanding for my love for jazz, which was condemned by the State as hidden enemy propaganda and decadent for youth. Although Mr Baldauf knew that I had no sympathy for the Hitler Youth and that my friends all agreed with me, I had the feeling during questioning that he was not against my point of view. I know Mr Baldauf as a good person, and many of my friends are of the same opinion.

A fudged photocopy of a letter dated 2 June 1947 from a Czech musician whose name is illegible, born in Prague in 1882 reads, in part:

. . . I was deported as a forced labourer to Germany after the closing of Prague University, where I was a philosophy student. I was lucky, I worked as a pianist in a dance orchestra . . . I met Mr Heinz Baldauf in his professional capacity. The orchestra consisted of Czechs who were all, like me, anti-Nazi. We did not like the music we were forced to play by the German police, and as often as possible we broke the rules. Mr Baldauf, who was our control officer, should have punished us when he heard that we were playing the forbidden swing music or Czech folk songs. But he did not. He sympathized with us. Sometimes he even requested a Czech folk song he liked very much. He was also aware of the fact that we Czechs had German girlfriends, which was strictly forbidden under punishment of concentration camps. My Czech colleagues all feel the same as I do. Mr Baldauf continually demonstrated his sympathy and friendship for us foreigners. It is perhaps redundant to point out that as a foreigner deported to Germany by force I was a confirmed enemy of the Nazi regime. I swear to this. (Signed.)

A letter from Dr Artur Schulder of Frankfurt:

I met Mr Baldauf in 1942 when I was caught by him and questioned for breaking some Nazi law I never quite understood. After three months I was freed for lack of proof. Even so, the three months were an incredible strain physically and psycho-logically, they were very difficult months. I thought all was lost ... All would have been lost if I had not had the incredible luck to deal with Mr Baldauf, who was very loyal to me and is a wonderful person. So I want to make the following statements. 1: Mr Baldauf never dealt with me in anything but a civilized tone, he never threatened me, never punished me. 2: He allowed me to dictate my statements into a machine by myself. This was essential for me to formulate my defence. 3: On every new day of questioning, he allowed me to make additions to my statements of the day before so that after reflecting for twenty-four hours I could add something in better form to help my defence. 4: He allowed my wife and once or twice my children to visit me, and he was kind to them. 5: After they freed me, 31 July 1942, he took the initiative – and my wife can verify it because she witnessed it – to convince his bosses, who were not at all sure of it, of my innocence . . . Mr Baldauf is what I consider a very special exception. After I was freed, one of his colleagues said to me, 'You were lucky to be dealing with a human being.' Baldauf said to him, 'Not so loud. That is not a compliment around here . . .'

Letter from Herr Peter Haas, Frankfurt, 29 August 1947:

I am the son of a Frankfurt lawyer who was murdered in 1923 for political reasons. My father was a Jew, I am a half-Jew. During the war I was questioned many times by the Gestapo and ended up in a concentration camp. I was in Granienburg and Drei Bergen. I was given the camp number 005994 . . . At the beginning of 1943, I had dealings with the criminally charged Heinz Baldauf, who was a Gestapo officer, in my mother's apartment in Frankfurt. I gave parties there for my young men and women friends and we danced to English records and listened to banned radio stations. Because they were my parties and because of my Jewish roots, I was the most in danger. It was forbidden for me to have contact with Aryan women for racial reasons. A neighbour denounced us to the police. One evening around eleven, all of a sudden lots of police officers invaded the apartment in the middle of one of our parties. Mr Baldauf was one of them. He searched the apartment in a proper manner. One of my guests, who was seventeen, was very arrogant but Mr Baldauf was not provoked. I was afraid because they found us listening to one of the forbidden radio stations. Mr Baldauf asked me to come into the next room and, looking me straight in the eye, he said, 'Mr Haas, you are a half-Jew. This could mean real trouble for you, so I will overlook the matter of the radio station, it will not be written into my report.' The result was that I was not punished and until today I am thankful for his humanity. As a concentration camp survivor I would not give Mr Baldauf, a Gestapo officer, my support if he was not worthy. I am prepared to swear to everything I have said.

Is it possible? A good Gestapo officer? A nice SS man?
'The SS was an elite corps,' Baldauf told me, ordering a second brandy and beer. 'You had to be at least 1.79m in height, be physically clean, have at least two sports medals, and a correct psychological bill of health. These were not thieves or gangsters. There were no locks on the lockers. It was considered an honour to be admitted into the service. I will not lie to you. I was not anti-Nazi, but I was still a human being.'
I asked Baldauf if he had worn a uniform on duty. He reached into his pocket, pulled out his wallet and from it two photos of

himself in uniform. He passed them around the table. 'He looks Jewish, don't you think?' Carlo asked me. Not to me. I wondered if he always carries those photos in his wallet. Or did he just put them there to show me? Weird either way. I suddenly had an image of all the men Baldauf's age walking on West German streets with such photos in their wallets. And I imagined weekly Gestapo veteran meetings in the Opel Stube. All the nice Gestapo officers. Baldauf ordered a third brandy and beer. I ordered another schnapps and beer.

He had been a soldier for a while before passing the SS test. He knew how much happy music meant to soldiers on home leave. That is why he had been tolerant of Otto and Carlo and the others who played jazz. But he had to draw the line between musicians and gangsters. He once slapped a 'brat' who said 'you can kiss my ass'. Later this kid testified against him in his Nürnberg trial. The testimony added six weeks to his sentence. He said: 'I could have sent that kid to jail, but I only slapped him.'

'What were you sentenced for?' I asked him.

'Pimps and whores,' he answered. 'I gave them trouble and they came back and testified against me.'

A moment of silence.

'In 1941 there was a national SS seminar in Berlin on the subject of how to enforce the banning of jazz. Different officers from different cities had different ideas. I was for leniency. I saw no real harm in it. I like jazz. I like to dance with my wife. Though jazz was banned there were no strict rules about its definition. It was up to each officer to interpret just what was jazz.'

A couple with a small child settled at a neighbouring table in the Opel Stube. Baldauf suggested we move into the empty back room. Ah ha! This was where the Gestapo veterans surely met. As we sat down he seemed to read my mind: 'I can understand how you would feel uncomfortable speaking to the Gestapo.'

You bet. Not even the past tense. He would not let me use my tape-recorder. He explained that a journalist had once lied about him and a million people read it. Later the paper printed a correction and only, maybe, a thousand read that. I pointed out that his reasoning was faulty. 'I have a bad memory,' I said. He said I could take notes.

'You could not sing in English, of course, that was a clear rule. But that is understandable, no? You could not sing in German during the war in America.'

'You could play Beethoven.'

That stopped him. He continued: 'Kids were stealing ration cards, money. Their fathers were in the army, their mothers worked. Somebody had to keep an eye on them. You know, I lost two brothers in the war.'

Was I supposed to feel sorry about that? Two dead Germans. Yes, maybe I should feel sorry. We ordered more boilermakers. He continued: 'One night there was a complaint from a waiter in a restaurant about a customer who said, "Hitler can lick my ass." '

There seemed to be a lot of talk about ass-licking in those days.

'I was obliged to investigate,' he continued. 'I took him in, he was sent away for three years. After the war he accused me of not only sending him to prison but beating him up so hard I knocked out three teeth. Well, I've seen this fellow's record and I happen to know that he already had false teeth when he was arrested. I confronted him with that through my lawyer. He said, "I guess I forgot." My sentence was reduced from eight to five years.

'You have to realize . . .' He hesitated as though conscious of stretching the limits of the believable: 'Look, if I was a Gestapo officer in Frankfurt, that meant I did not have to go to the Russian front. Better Frankfurt than Stalingrad.'

That strikes me as just crazy enough to believe. I tend to believe Baldauf believes it. Join the Gestapo as a sort of draft-dodge. Though it does sound like your cosmic cop-out, it is nevertheless true that Germans went to great lengths avoiding the Eastern front. In *French and Germans, Germans and French*, Richard Cobb writes:

The officer in charge of relations with the Bordeaux press told his friends among the journalists that nothing could have upset him more than to have to leave the city especially if it were to go east; Lille was not much sought after but even it was infinitely better than the Russian front. At quite a humble level, the case of Haefs – the limpet-like official who had attached himself to Radio Paris, following it, like a rejected suitor, from Paris to Nancy, thence to Belfort and Sigmaringen – could no doubt be reproduced over and over again. For Haefs, there *had* to be a Radio Paris, however useless it might be once it had set up tent in Germany, because it was the alibi that protected him from the Eastern front.

Baldauf went on after one more brandy and beer: 'My chief, a lieutenant, sometimes he would question me why I allowed certain music and I would tell him it was easier to control people by allowing this music to be played. They congregate around it and I can keep my eye on them. I'd rather know where the subversives are. But really I liked the music.' He whistled a strain from 'Take The "A" Train'.

So here we have a nice jazz-loving SS man who was only in that feared and brutal corps as a draft-dodge, and never harmed a guiltless soul. Yet the heartless Allies sent him to prison for five years. 'It was a hard thing for me to carry,' he said, turning sour now. 'When I was released I did not have the right to have a driver's licence, I could not have a telephone. I had a wife and two children, I worked hard labour from nine to nine for ninety-two pfennings an hour. Then slowly slowly, little by little, small...' He made a rising motion with his hand: 'It is good here. If you work life is good here. I worked my way up with a coffee company and when I retired there were thirty-two workers under my responsibility.'

As we paid the bill, he said to me: 'You must get a lot of mail from all over the world. I save stamps. Could you send me some stamps?'

Outside, waiting for a taxi, weaving from alcohol and a wind that had suddenly sprung up, Baldauf said: 'Now you know that all SS men were not beasts who grabbed you by the collar and sent you to the concentration camps.' He almost fell because I ducked when he playfully grabbed my collar.

9
Bad Connection

On a bend in the river near Fontainebleau, where the road ends, hard not to get lost looking for, Samois-sur-Seine is one of those exurban towns that might be described as 'unspoiled' had it not been artificially preserved by restrictive zoning. Surrounded by the Fontainebleau forest, it is basically for those who run things, with a smattering of burned-out rockers, smashed lackeys, eccentric fishermen, Gypsies and barge people.

Houses and gardens are strung along the river road and up a hillside on unpaved paths between the few through streets. The town goes back to the seventeenth century and the architecture is a melange of Louis XIV, Mussolini-modern and transplanted Americana. The variety is united by benign neglect, the French version of those Dutch and Swiss neighbourhoods where million-aires live understated lifestyles to fool the tax collector and second-storey men.

A single-engine plane flew under heavy clouds towing a banner: 'Festival Django Reinhardt, Samois/Seine'. Django lived his last years and died here. He is the only non-American in the jazz pantheon with Louis Armstrong, Duke Ellington, Billie Holiday, Charlie Parker, John Coltrane and the others; all Afro-Americans. He was a Gypsy, a close call; these are unwelcome tribes.

We checked into the 'Country Club Hotel, *avec vue sur Seine*', which has walls so thin you can just about see through them. Hell, you can just about see through me. My body reminds my wife of Dachau. 'Your thighs. You've got no thighs left,' France exclaimed just the other night. This book refuses to stay in the past.

Bad luck. How else to explain rain leaking through the roof of our new ground-floor apartment, which is in a six-storey building?

Take my word for it. We sleep under a thin floor on which two children ride square-wheeled tricycles. The cheap elevator installed to raise controlled rents to expel unwanted Arabs on upper floors has a motor with an angry growl, and we have invisible walls of our own.

I called France's office extension last week: '*Allo*. Henry Pecked here. Remember me? Good old Hen?'

'*Qui?!*'

The ministry where she works is a nest of snakes run by bureaucrats who treat human beings like . . . snakes. Her eleven-month contract dissolved into none at all, reappeared as two and now for some reason they're talking nine. Number nine. They are more like sentences than contracts.

She has been transferred to four departments in a year – different tasks, new co-workers, other offices. 'I don't know who I am any more,' she cried on my shoulder. She cries in the morning, in her sleep, in the bathtub, cooking, at work too I presume.

'Don't let them break your spirit.'

'It's already broken.'

One morning when the elevator growled and the square wheels turned at the same time, France just threw back her head and let out a howl. I could feel one kilo pack its bag and leave right then and there. So when a reasonably modulated voice on the other side of the wall in the Country Club Hotel sounded as though it came from our bed, I tried to drown it out: 'Look at the beautiful view of the Seine,' I said. But I knew better. It was a weekend that would be drowned out.

'*Quel bummer!*' my son said.

Two banks make the water between them twice as interesting as the sea. The sea steals half a view. Long banks discourage acute concentrations of people and vehicles. Rivers turn and twist and the towns on them are often cuddly and tucked away. With little wind and no waves, there are no surfers with their flippers, thick hair and exposed aggressive young curves. 'I love rivers,' I always say. 'You always say that,' says my wife, who loves the sea.

I took a walk with my son, who loves seas and rivers and mountains too. The soccer ball he dribbled along the river road between the Country Club Hotel and the town landed on a lawn.

'Keep that ball off my lawn,' a lady shouted from her window.

A plaque on one simple attached house just like the others on a narrow street proclaimed: 'Here lived and died the guitarist and composer Django Reinhardt, 1910–1953', with a drawing of Django playing guitar. Robbie sat down on the curb and tried to copy the drawing but the street was narrow and cars kept honking at him to pull in his legs.

Gypsies were camped up in the *haute ville* behind the main square, next to the cemetery where Django is buried. Gypsies camp here every year for the Django Reinhardt festival. Lines of laundry hung between trailers parked amidst a colourful array of battered automobiles. Mattresses and children's shoes were spread out to dry on the lawn even though it had been raining all week and the grass was muddy. People who look, well, different from you and I sat on folding chairs roasting chickens on open fires and drinking wine, cases of which stood on folding tables. Everything seemed to be folding around here.

Gypsies take to guitars, a good travelling instrument. I keep meeting Gypsies who claim to be Django Reinhardt's cousin. And I keep hearing good guitar players. Two Gypsies – Maurice Ferret and Joseph Pouvil, I later learned – were strumming between a trailer and a pile of mattresses.

'Papa, what's a Gypsy?'

'Well, son, I'm glad you asked . . .'

Defined: 'Member of a wandering race of Indian origin, a Romani (Rom)', the Gypsy people began leaving India about 1,500 years ago. They prefer to be called Roms, but the world knows them as Gypsies, and they often lapse and refer to themselves that way. They moved away in successive waves from local wars – disunited, vulnerable, small tribes travelling with their animals.

They hold on to a loose body of religious belief based on Hinduism, although practical Gypsies adopt the religion of whatever country they are in. Some are Christian and Muslim at the same time in places where that makes sense. The family – more an extended family, a clan – comes first. The Gypsy idea of hell on earth is to live in the same house and work for somebody else all their lives. They prefer day labour, sporadic small enterprise in which they can preserve some semblance of freedom

– asphalting, cherry-picking, collecting scrap.

The Gypsies reached Greece around the eighth century, western Europe during the Middle Ages. Europeans thought they were from Egypt, thus 'Gypsy'. Their roots were on the road, and in any case there was little space for them to settle. Earlier migrations had already staked out the best territory. They were forced to move on the fringes of established society and their nomadic tendency was reinforced. Pariahs, forever on foreign soil, they were often forced to steal to stay alive. It was also difficult to take baths. They were expelled ('punishment for Gypsies and beggars entering this district') and slaughtered ('by taking the life of a Gypsy the defendant did not act against the policy of the state').

Dropped out as they have been for centuries, Gypsies are compared to hippies (both called 'unclean' in a society where neatness counts); being all diaspora, to Jews (*'Gaja'*, Romani for non-Gypsy, bears an uncanny resemblance to *'Goye'*, Yiddish for non-Jew).

There are over five million Gypsies in Europe. Legend has it that a Gypsy smithy forged the nails which crucified Christ – worse, sold them. There have been heavy dues to pay. Half a million died in concentration camps and the measure of their alienation can be gauged by the fact that many survivors did not feel safe enough to surface for a census. Gypsy Auschwitz survivors refused to provide details about their families.

In *The Destiny of Europe's Gypsies* Kenrick and Puxon write:

They were reluctant to impart any information even for indemnification claims which could be used to trace and detail relations because they suspected persecution would recommence . . . There could be no guarantee that the claim forms would not be scrutinized by police agencies. Some of the single survivors and orphaned children soon fell into difficulties under the military occupation authorities and the new German civil law. Anyone who lost their displaced person's card or whose records in the UN relief agency archives had been misplaced or who had served a term in prison for any offence could be refused papers they needed after release. In this situation when next picked up by the police, they were liable to deportation on a court order or would simply be told on police authority to quit

Germany. Some Gypsies, unable to obtain admission to another state, were reimprisoned and served further terms . . .

Not one Gypsy witness testified during the Nürnberg trials.

Robbie and I walked down to Chez Fernand, where Django used to drink, on the river where Django used to fly-fish, for an interview with Jean-François Robinet, the town's dynamic young mayor. A journalist and jazz fan, he started these yearly homages over the objections of his constituency. 'The people here did not know Django as a musician,' he said. 'Or even as a Gypsy. He was known as a billiard champion. In 1950 he beat the Fontainebleau billiard team single-handedly for the Département championship. And they knew him as a fisherman. One year, it was unlike him, he fished out of season. "I can't wait," he explained. "I'll be dead by the season." He was.'

Robinet told me that certain influential residents detest the festival because it attracts Gypsies, hippies and noisy bearded people: 'They don't have any real respect for Django, this genius who chose to live among them. But I do. And too bad for them; they voted for me.'

It began to drizzle in the late afternoon. France joined us and we moved inside the cafe. I had reserved a table on the terrace of the nearby restaurant which overlooks the barge where tonight's music would be. The mayor introduced me to a dark-skinned man wearing a jacket capelike over his shoulders with a wide-brimmed white fedora on his head: 'Monsieur Rafael, this is Mike . . .' he had forgotten my last name. 'He's writing a book about Django.'

'Not exactly.' I started to correct him: 'Actually the book is about . . .'

M Rafael could have been around sixty. He was thin but muscular, one eyelid drooped, and a dandy cigar danced in his mouth. He looked Sicilian, but in these circumstances I doubted it. The diamond in one tooth was perhaps a recompense for the empty space beside it. The missing top tooth and a jutting jaw made him resemble the bulldog on a leash at his feet.

'*C'est intéressante, ça.*' M Rafael tipped back the fedora. '*Moi, je suis le cousin de Django.*'

'He looks just like his dog,' Robbie whispered.

'Shh.'

There were umbrellas over the tables on the terrace of the restaurant so we sat outside despite the drizzle. The mayor was in conference as Rafael walked away down the *quai* in the direction of the cemetery. I had made an appointment with him for noon tomorrow. Robbie lost control of his soccer ball and it rolled into the Seine. 'I already told you seventy-five times . . .' I ground my teeth. A festival grip fished it out, flashing a friendly smile. 'Never let your balls get wet.' France and Robbie smiled back. They have nice smiles. I did not smile. I have a nice smile too.

The drizzle turned to rain and then it poured and the umbrellas were thick enough only for sun. We were soon soaked. The couples at the next table held their glasses in the air until the rain filled them and then they proposed toasts. Between the rainwater, they drank champagne. They were young and happy and drunk and made lots of noise. They knocked their umbrella down. It made a lot of noise and broke a few dishes and they laughed loudly until everyone else on the terrace laughed with them.

'Assholes!' I muttered. The concert was cancelled.

We decided I'd run for the car and come back with it; no need for all of us to get wet. I slipped jumping over a puddle and tore the knee of my jeans. There was no blood but the shock took my breath away. The day before I had withdrawn 35,000 francs from the bank, the final payment for building our new apartment. That took my breath away too.

I drove back to the temporary barriers that sealed off the town's central area from traffic. Even with the wipers on high it was hard to see the road. My little family was not there. I waited five minutes. After a snappy salute, a gendarme asked me to move on. I explained that it was raining very hard and I did not want my wife, who has a cold, and young child to get wet. 'Move on,' he said. My press card did not impress him.

It took ten minutes to drive around the elaborate one-way system, come back down the hill and find a legal parking space farther down the road. But then Robbie and France appeared by the barrier, so I pulled up.

'Where have you been?'

'What took you so long?'

As I made a U-turn to avoid the one-way system, the gendarme appeared again, saluted again and asked for my papers. He said the

U-turn was illegal and our seat belts were not fastened, though there was no traffic and the hotel was only half a kilometre away. I waited near his window in the wet wind as he filled out tickets. Robbie brought an umbrella and kept me company. The gendarme asked for France's identity card and Robbie ran to our car to ask her for it. She was not giving it to him. He looked at me nervously. She slammed our door getting out.

'You have no right to ask for my papers,' she said to the gendarme. 'I wasn't driving. *Des salauds!* What is this?! Nazi Germany?'

'I'll talk to the mayor about this!' I felt hot blood well. 'We're guests.'

'As you wish, *monsieur.*'

'Please . . .' Robbie whispered. 'He'll put us in jail.' He was very frightened.

M Rafael appeared, a 'Django Djazz' button pinned to his double-breasted raincoat, also hanging capelike.

'What's the trouble?' he asked. We told him. 'May I see those?' He took the tickets, read them and motioned us back to our car. We watched him speak to the gendarme. Then he came and leaned in our window. 'Do not worry. I will take care of it. Sleep well.'

The voice on the other side of the wall was saying: 'You should work on your backhand.'

The Sunday-morning memorial service for Django was conducted by Guy De Fatto, a bassist turned priest, in a beautiful refurbished seventeenth-century municipal hall. The priest was flanked, accompanied and spelled by Ferret and Pouvil playing songs associated with Django on acoustic guitars.

'Music is the source of life,' De Fatto began. 'Music has always represented life for me. I discovered God through music. When I played with Django in the caves of St Germain des Pres, we created life together. Django helped me discover this greater life, the life beyond human life, he brought me without knowing it to someone who was even a greater creator than himself.

'God gave the gift of music to certain men, certainly he gave it to Gypsies. Then one day Django Reinhardt was born and his gift was even larger. Man has not always used his God-given creativity as well as Django. Man has made bombs with which to kill other men.

'We must believe in life. Before, I believed only in music, I lived for music. Music was my religion. It was somehow holy to be able to express what we had inside of us . . .'

The two Gypsy guitarists began to play 'Nuages'. They were accompanied by the sound of raindrops on the roof. 'Perhaps God wishes to make music with his own clouds,' said the priest, smiling.

'Django's music is still alive. I do not really know if he is in what we call "the sky" but I am sure that his spirit lives and that we are in communication with him. Last night I dreamed that I telephoned Django . . .'

The two guitarists played 'Manoir de Mes Rêves'.

'One day I'm going to end up in trouble yelling at cops,' France whispered. 'I don't know, I can't control it. How long do you think we'd have stayed out of prison in Nazi Germany?'

Robbie was playing with a piece of Lego on the floor.

'. . .I said to him,' the priest continued. ' "Django, you who know clouds so well, please ask them to be kind to us today." But I do not know if he heard me. The connection was bad.'

10
Occupation Blues

A Dutchman named Henk Niesen, Jr wrote an article called
'Occupation Blues' in the British magazine *Jazz Forum* in 1946.
Wearing earplugs and a sleep-mask, France wound a leg around
what was left of my thigh while I read it. It goes something like
this.

There was never any good jazz in Holland – or in any European
country for that matter. Jazz is a very subtle art practised only by
a special breed of American Negroes.

None the less in 1939 there were some joints in Amsterdam
where you could hear a pale imitation because the great
Coleman Hawkins had played there. But Bean had seen the
clouds gathering and took a steamer home. After five days in
May the fighting was over and everything appeared to return to
normal. Everybody played whatever they liked and it looked
like we were going to jitterbug rather than sing the blues
through the occupation. But then Seyss-Inquart, the great
traitor, banned English and American songs.

But still everybody played them. Freddy Johnson played in a
little cafe with a trio consisting of a drummer and a tenor player,
both not bad. And with Freddy himself in top form, singing and
tickling the ivories, it was eldorado. The place was so crowded
that it was difficult to find a chair. And there we heard Freddy
play the latest hits from the banned English radio. I spent many
afternoons and evenings there in the most happy circumstances,
forgetting all about the war.

Tension gradually increased. The Jewish drummerboy vanished with the first pogroms. In his place came a coloured drummer

from Surinam, thus making a Negro trio, as the tenor sax and owner of the cafe hailed also from that place in the western hemisphere.

The going in 1940 and the first half of 1941 was still good, though at the time we thought that it was already bad. There were no cigarettes, or incredibly bad ones, and those that were smokable vanished into the black market. There was nearly no gin and the beer was not what it used to be. Still there was good music and the Chinese continued preparing their fine dishes. I can still see Freddy Johnson eating his 'Bami' or 'Foe Yong Hay' with that big smile of his. 'This is the only thing you can do now with your money,' he said to my wife. 'Eat and drink.'

And we certainly did. Those were unforgettable days and I learned a lot from Freddy. From 1934 until 1941 Freddy Johnson showed me the way through the jazz labyrinths. Freddy knew all the great soloists personally, he had played with Benny Carter, Hawkins, Rex, Jimmy Harrison and lots of others. His critical sense was sublime; he knew how jazz should be played. He knew how to swing a band and write a first-class arrangement. Another pianist substituted for him one evening when Freddy was giving a concert somewhere else. When the worthy Mr Johnson entered the cafe again, late in the evening, in the very middle of a song, he took over the piano and the whole atmosphere changed at once, it became highly charged. That was Freddy.

Then came 7 December 1941 – Japan had attacked Pearl Harbor. The Nazis interned all Americans and Freddy Johnson was transported to Germany. The Nazis in Amsterdam were very happy to be able to get rid of this 'uppity nigger'. Willie Lewis had already escaped to Switzerland. That was the end of jazz in Holland.

I heard that Freddy lived fairly comfortably in a German prisoners' camp until 1944 when he was exchanged against German prisoners in American hands and went back to New York to eat 'Bami' while we all starved.

Sure, we had all sorts of Dutch bands that played American numbers camouflaged with Dutch lyrics to fool the Germans, but no real jazz any more. The Ramblers, Ernst Van't Hoff, Dick Willebrant; they all played nice arrangements pleasantly enough, but I was not interested. It was not the real thing. Why bother?

'Jazz regulations' were invented by an official of the Kultur-kammer, a certain Gilbert, who used to be a jazz critic and who ordered that no music with after-beat, Negro vibrato and so on should be played. Imagine what kind of people spend their time troubling with such nonsense!

There was a boom in Hawaiian orchestras that played 'Hula Hula' and it was all nonsense but great fun. Gradually there was less and less music. Only people with lots of money could afford the bars and cafes, mainly black-marketeers and they were not agreeable company. They shouted themselves hoarse drinking gin at five to ten guilders apiece, and thought they were having a marvellous time. The lights of the city were still burning then. But after the failure of the landing at Arnhem, all the lights went out and there remained only a big black world without any music at all.

11
Django, Maccaferri and Paul

By the time I met M Rafael at noon, the Sunday-afternoon concert had also been cancelled. 'Django would have thought it was very funny.' He was smoking a Dunhill now. 'It rains every year for his festival. He never went outside at all if he could help it.'

'I thought he liked to fish.'

'Oh, that was just so he could goof off and nobody would bother him about it.'

'Did you know him well?'

'Of course. He was my cousin.' He went behind the bar, came back with a battered guitar and began to strum 'Lover Man'.

'I remember when I first heard he died, it was in a pub in Oxford. Somebody came in with the *Daily Mirror* and said: "Pity about Django dying." I'll always remember that pub, like you always remember where you heard that Kennedy was assassinated.

'I left for Paris the next day to see his brother Joseph. Cousin Joseph was a beautiful guitar player, but Django overshadowed him. Django made him carry his guitar. Joseph was always a step behind, carrying Django's guitar. Joseph considered it an honour.

'Joseph was living in a little caravan on a fairground at the end of the metro line. The caravan was full of cousins, there were big fires outside and dogs prowling about. Django's violin was hanging on the wall, and a couple of his paintings. They were terrible, awful, he was a bad painter. The violin was wrapped in one of Django's silk scarves. Later, Naguine, Django's widow, gave the scarf to Stephane Grappelli. It's got a red border and musical notes on it. Stephane still wraps his violin in Django's scarf before he puts it in the case.'

Rafael was wearing a polyester jogging jacket, with 'Bob Seger World Tour' on the back. Somebody later told me that he worked for the Deuxième Bureau, the French secret service. He looked like Mafia to me.

'Stephane and Django didn't get on very well. The quintet would get a job at some posh place and the local Gypsies would hear about it and when Stephane went to their dressing-room – Django always made sure they had fancy dressing-rooms – all these Gypsies would be in there. They'd been out stealing chickens and they'd pluck and cook them. Once there was no stove so they just started burning the furniture.

'Stephane never liked Gypsies. They loved to give him trouble. Even now, when he plays in the south of Germany a gang of Gypsies is always sitting right down front. There are a lot of Gypsies around the Black Forest. They come to send him up, but also there's some real respect because of his connection with Django. They say hello in the dressing-room afterwards. When he sees them coming, Stephane screams, "Lock the door, look out for your shirts."

'Stephane is careful with his money; Django was a spender. He was always ordering rounds of Calvados or apple cider for anybody who happened to be in the cafe. Also Stephane is, well, uncomfortable around women. Django loved to cat. When he saw a bird he liked from the bandstand, he'd play his guitar right *at* her.'

Rafael said 'cat' and 'bird' in English. What was this Franglais mixture of hipster and Chelsea slang? Why would a Gypsy refer to Gypsies in the third person? And where had he learned to play 'Lover Man'?

'Beautiful, isn't it?' he said, holding up the guitar to admire it. 'Early model Maccaferri. Must be worth five thousand dollars by now.'

Mario Maccaferri was a Sicilian classical guitarist who invented a way of building a special soundboard which curved in two directions enabling the player to get a particularly penetrating tone out of an acoustic instrument. In the beginning he made only a few for himself, then a few hundred of the cutaway type Django used and by now that model has the status of a Guarneri violin. Though Django played a key role in the success of that model, Maccaferri did not have a high opinion of jazz musicians in general and they never met. Later Maccaferri founded a company in the US that manufactured over nine million Arthur Godfrey model plastic ukuleles.

'A lot of people think they have Django's Maccaferri,' Rafael continued. 'Diz Disley over in London. Barney Kessel claims some Gypsies presented him with an old Maccaferri and said, "Here you are, this belonged to Django, he would have wanted you to have it." Les Paul says that some Gypsies came to give him Django's guitar.

'Les came to Paris once and asked me for Django's telephone number. I said, "If you find it let me know; he's disappeared." He gave me half of a $100 bill and said I'd get the other half when I found Django. Two nights later they were jamming together. Django told Les that he could not keep up with the electric guitar, it was driving him nuts, kept running away from him. Les invented the solid-body electric guitar and he felt sort of responsible. Django looked real bad – thin, big bags under his eyes . . . bad. "It's just a different technique," Les said.

'Django died a few months later. Right here in Samois, as you know. While he was on his deathbed, he told Babik, "Don't ever play the guitar. You'll never be as good as your father."

'Babik? Little Joey, his son. Actually, it's Babik who has Django's Maccaferri. He used to be wild, had trouble with the law, passing bad cheques I think. He's settled down now, but Babik used to drive his mother to distraction, always getting into trouble.

'Django had two Maccaferris. One was cracked and they put it on top of his coffin when he was buried. Babik has the other one. So you see this is Gypsies for you. They'll tell you anything. Don't misunderstand, I love my people. But let me give you a tip, you seem like a nice young man; never believe anything a Gypsy tells you.'

There was a moment of silence as he pulled out another Dunhill. 'Basically they are all anarchists. They won't have all this bureaucracy stuck on them. They are outsiders, absolutely free people. I'm going down to Spain this week . . .' He began to play in Flamenco style on the Maccaferri . . . if indeed it really was one. 'A lot of Gypsies play Flamenco guitar in Spain. They pick grapes and live in old buses sprayed with silver paint with big TV antennas. I can't live that way myself. All they want out of life is . . . who was the American politician who got fired for saying that about Negroes? . . . a tight cunt, a loose pair of shoes and a warm place to shit. That's really not too bad, but I want more myself. A few families camp by the sea and all of a sudden there are old cars everywhere. They tear them to pieces, sell the parts and the scrap metal and move on. Terrible mess. If you want to know more it will cost you one hundred dollars.'

After my surprise at the sudden transition, I figured the price was cheap enough. France and I each had a 500-franc note. I gave them to him.

'No dollars?'

I shrugged: 'No. But keep the change.' It was about 100 francs over at the time.

He laughed: 'What change? The dollar will be ten in six months.' It was.

I had been meaning to ask him: 'What were you doing in Oxford?'

'I had a foundation grant to write a history of the Roms. I was doing research. I have a degree from the University of Bucharest. They'll give anybody a grant if you know how to talk to them. You should have a grant for your book. If you want I can tell you how to deal with foundations. My grant was twenty thousand dollars. I will tell you for only two fifty. Cheap, no?'

I said I'd think about it, we talked some more and he wrote down his phone number. It turned out to be a muffler-repair shop in Montreuil. And not too long ago we received a summons from the police to pay the tickets he 'took care of' in Samois.

12
The Guitar with a Human Voice

In the winter of 1920, a dirty Gypsy child was begging between a horse-meat butcher and a used-shoe stall on the Kremlin-Bicétre market. He was just like any other begging Gypsy child, except that he played a battered banjo.

Little Django Reinhardt played his banjo here every Sunday. His younger brother Joseph passed a hat. Already you could hear something, well, bizarre. Passages from 'Au Claire de la Lune' alternated with out-of-tune aleatoric clusters like round-the-bend Stravinsky. He seemed hypnotized by his strings. It was as though someone else was fingering them. If you had ever been to New Orleans you might have recognized a few phrases that sounded like the blues, which was even more bizarre because Django had never been there. He played Romanian folk songs with his uncle in a small cafe on Saturdays.

The two boys moved into a bistro, staying near the door as usual, ready to leave fast before being thrown out. An accordionist named Guerino, sipping his habitual after-mass absinthe, invited them to sit down with him at a table. 'Can you play the "Blue Danube"? I love waltzes.'

Sensing loose change, Django played a waltz with more courage than finesse. It even sounded a little like the 'Blue Danube'.

Guerino heard something. He asked Django where he lived and the boy led him to his caravan parked near Porte d'Italie. He had been born in that caravan, while passing through Belgium. By the time he was five he had travelled 3,000 miles in it, with his mother and a succession of fathers.

With the mother's blessing, Guerino offered Django his first professional engagement for the following Sunday in a dancehall called La Montagne, rue de la Montagne Sainte-Genviève. It was an 'in' place frequented by students, journalists, weirdos and adventurers. Pay was ten francs a session. A pack of cigarettes cost ninety centimes at the time, about the same as a glass of beer. It seemed like a lot of money just for playing the banjo, which he did all day long for nothing anyway.

He never had to 'learn' music. He just started to play it, played it ten hours a day, fingers swollen and sometimes bleeding by the end, played music without 'knowing' a note. He could not read or write, either music or words and he would never learn. He only went to school for one day in his life. Later he would avoid the metro because he could not read the station signs.

A photograph taken of him in La Montagne three years later shows what resembles a Harlem street hustler preoccupied by major capers. Or maybe an oriental prince. Tall for his age, thin and natty, his hair is slicked back, he is wearing a blue serge suit, a tweed vest, starched white shirt, an elegantly knotted tie and shiny black shoes..He had just been awarded first prize in a banjo contest.

The 'Friends of the Accordion' threw a banquet. Answering a request, Guerino launched into 'Crystal Pearl', a virtuoso exercise not for just anyone. Django accompanied him eyes closed, with enthusiasm. Guerino leaned over and said, 'You've got it, little man.'

Django had never played 'Crystal Pearl' before. He anticipated the next step, remembered every step after only once and he soon owned it. He began slowly, bending notes here and there, vibrating others. He found harmonic subtleties and melodic variations he could never have defined. Why bother? They had been found. Later Guerino criticized him for fooling around with the melody.

Already, Django liked to disappear. They were not exactly binges, though he also liked wine and women. They might more accurately be defined as an affirmation of free will. He played poker, *belote*, billiards, music of course, went to sleep at dawn or not at all. He slept when he was sleepy, whenever and wherever that might be.

When he was only fifteen, he did not come home for three days. Finally, tiptoeing into the caravan, he kissed his mother, who was called Négros and who had not slept for three nights. 'I looked for you all over Paris,' she reproached him.

He sat down at the foot of her bed, took out a guitar (which had by then replaced the banjo) and began to play a song. 'Do you like this song?' he asked her.

Guerino was not the same without Django. He too had not slept. He accused Négros of inadequate discipline. She was furious at his interference in Gypsy family matters and approved when Django decided to take a job with Guerino's competitor Alexander.

Django had just acquired a bad habit. Taxis. Worse – limousines. There was something about him that inspired a chauffeur's confidence. He already played the role of prince well, and would learn to play it better. He seemed so removed, above it all, to have important matters on his mind. Do not bother me about mere money. He hired Packards, Panhards, Citroëns and Rolls-Royces by the hour or day. More money could always come. All he had to do was pick up his guitar. It was so *easy*. Only the occasional driver would turn him down, spotting something fishy about the grey spats and the fancy rings, the hair just a bit too shiny.

By the age of eighteen, accompanying Alexander was beginning to bore him. It was *too* easy. Backing up these vaudeville clowns was not very princely. He was not particularly receptive when the xylophone artist Carlito asked him to play accompaniment on four sides for the Idéal label. 'Five hundred francs isn't too bad,' Carlito insisted. 'Idéal records are sold everywhere. No telling where it can lead.'

True, it would pay for a lot of limousines, and he had a woman now and she was pregnant. He lived with her and his mother in the same caravan. His mother called it 'that sardine can'.

When the records came out he bought a second caravan for his mother. For a while after the baby was born, Django came home after work like a family man. He was to have a succession of 'wives' to whom he was not officially married and to whom his unfaithfulness did not basically take the form of other women, although he had them too. He was just out all the time.

Like his mother, the wives sold lace and artificial flowers door-to-door and in the markets around the gates of Paris. Otherwise they stayed home and waited for Django.

British bandleader Jack Hylton made a special trip to Paris to hear him, but he arrived on one of those nights when Django had decided to disappear. It was not even a decision. He was just somewhere else. In the middle of a billiard match perhaps, or fishing. There was enough money for today. The guitar was just another rod or cue. It was all the same anyway, just fingers.

Hylton came back the following night (they always came back), 2 November 1928. He was wearing a tuxedo, a fur-collared coat and he had a beautiful woman on each arm. He was smoking a fat, sweet-smelling cigar and the women smelled fine too. 'I came last night but you weren't here,' he said.

'I play when it pleases me.' Django inhaled the cigar and the women. He was playing very very well that night.

'Your playing pleases *me* very much.'

Django stared as Hylton flashed a fat bankroll paying the bill. He said nothing. An apache dancer named Bobby Lapaze once said, 'Django only speaks whenever he loses an eye.'

'My orchestra plays jazz,' Hylton said, with pride. Django did not know what that was.

'Good guitar players are rare in England,' said Hylton, and they made an appointment to sign a contract for the following afternoon. This was one appointment he would be on time for. Be on time tomorrow and he would have a bankroll, a fat cigar and a beautiful woman on each arm.

Entering the caravan that night, he stumbled over a bouquet of artificial flowers. His wife lit a candle for him. The caravan was filled with artificial flowers his wife and her friends had made for a funeral tomorrow. During the night, the candle set fire to the flowers and the caravan burned. Django was taken to a hospital, where doctors wanted to amputate his badly scorched left leg. He refused, Django did not trust doctors. Two weeks later he became the father of a baby boy.

He could no longer play the guitar because his left, fretboard, hand looked as though it had been squeezed in a vice and stepped on. He favoured it, taking care of the child during the year it took him to learn to walk again. 'Poor kid,' he would say. 'You have a cripple for a father.'

Shock cut to the sunny Mediterranean port of Toulon, 1929. Tanned but starving, nineteen-year-old Django Reinhardt was learning how to play the guitar without using the paralysed ring- and little fingers of his fretboard hand.

He learned to drag the crippled fingers along the strings. All he did was practise, eat and sleep – mostly practise. The catastrophe became an asset; he used his paralysed fingers to dampen strings, found cross-fingerings which avoided frenzied runs, learned leaner voicings out of necessity. He was finding ways to use his thumb to play hitherto unplayable octave passages for which he would later be famous. The legendary Afro-American guitarist Wes Montgomery studied Django's 'crippled' technique to develop his own famous octave style.

Django and his brother Joseph, also playing guitar now, were busking in Toulon cafes. They wore the only clothes they owned. Django's guitar had no case. Joseph carried it for him. Princes do not carry guitars, they play them. Django did not care about having a guitar case. He never even thought about the instrument when he wasn't playing it. He would just put it in a corner and if Joseph forgot to pick it up, there it would stay. He never put it in the repair shop. If it broke he'd play it anyway and when it became unplayable he'd buy or steal another one. When a string broke, it would just stay broken until Joseph strung another.

Django would not fix himself either. He avoided dentists if he had a toothache. He did not trust *Gajo* repairers and he certainly preferred to play broken guitars than deal with fixing them. In 1953, he would die of a cerebral haemorrhage at the age of forty-three because he refused to see a *Gajo* doctor about the pain in his head.

He and Joseph slept on the beach near Toulon. The two of them had just up and left Paris and their women. No warning, no plans. Django only knew he had to go into the woodshed and that would be easier in the sun. *Gajo* often accused Django of being indolent, insolent, irresponsible, intolerant, arrogant, childish. But he was actually more child*like*, living for the moment, volatile; you could never tell what he was going to do next.

Stephane Grappelli says that whenever Django saw a George Raft movie, he'd imitate George Raft as he walked out. He loved the big bankrolls gangsters pulled out of their pockets and when he had money he'd tie the bills up in a rubber band and take out the entire wad paying for coffee or cigarettes. He could never be bothered to go and put the money in a bank, he'd just have this wad, hundreds of thousands of francs sometimes, usually noticeably smaller in the morning than the evening before.

Jean Cocteau described him: 'the guitar that laughs, that cries, that speaks, the guitar with a human voice', and as a 'proud hunted beast'. Erik Satie said he was 'a black sorcerer bringing some soul to white audiences'.

Note 'black', and 'soul', two words later to be closely associated with jazz, a style of music Django was about to discover.

Emil Savitry, a Toulonais painter, was sipping his evening pastisse with his friend Poffi, a guitar teacher. Poffi had heard them before: 'The one with the crippled hand is extraordinary, don't you think? He's a strange one. So quiet, so . . . different. They play all night for bouillabaisse and beer. They survive from day to day. It doesn't seem to bother them. I don't think they know any other way.'

Savitry invited the Reinhardts for a spaghetti dinner and then to his studio. He had some records he wanted them to hear. Eureka! It was like one of those old Hollywood flashes of inspiration. A bulb lights up. 'That's it,' exclaims the star.

Listening to Louis Armstrong, Duke Ellington and Earl Hines, Django sat like a coiled animal blinded by the sun. He closed his eyes, bent an ear towards the speaker. For the first time he understood his own musicality. He had found a family, new brothers. Gypsies were the niggers of Europe anyway. And wasn't his mother named Négros? Sweating, in a sort of trance, he finally stood up and said: 'The guitar player behind Louis is out of tune.'

He could do it better. He could be the best.

The information about Django's early life has come from interviews with Louis Vola, Joseph Reinhardt, Diz Disley, Jean Sablon, Stephane Grappelli and others, and from a series of excellent articles in *Jazz* magazine by Yves Salgues.

In a piece entitled: 'Notes and Digression on a Solo by Django Reinhardt', Paul Andréota describes his playing:

The more I listen to it ['Sandman', with Dicky Wells], the more I sense in it a disembodied spirit, bounding, doing what it pleases, and like a dream dancer, going wherever it pleases without ever finding the slightest obstacle to its fantasy. The melody goes for a stroll, meets some notes which entertain it, tarries there a while, goes on a while, returns, rediscovers the straightaway, only to break loose again . . . A young fool remarked to me one day, 'He makes his guitar talk.' This perfectly stupid cliché assumes an astonishing significance if one just switches it around: 'He talks guitar.' For it's not the instrument playing; the instrument no longer exists. Django swallowed it a long time ago . . . And above all one sees that impish smile of Django's when playing, as if he were saying, 'You know that's really not bad, but wait a second, you ain't seen nothing yet.' And then at the end he gets angry, he's fed up with all this delicateness. Suddenly he becomes brutal. Magnificent.

The brothers moved in with Savitry, who found them work in a club called Le Coq Hardi where they wore tuxedos Savitry bought for them. Steady, well-paid work carried Django's generosity to byzantine proportions. He bought rounds for Corsican gangsters, neighbourhood toughs, Occitan farmers; for sailors, musicians and Gypsies. He had handbills printed: 'Django Reinhardt is throwing a party to which you are invited. Please notify the Cafe de Lyon of your acceptance forty-eight hours in advance.'

Making money cost him so little. He played with such easy intoxication, no chemicals required. It was so much fun it was almost like stealing.

The Palm Beach Casino was opening a fancy new cabaret in nearby Cannes. Impresario Leon Voltera wanted a jazz band. It was, after all, the Jazz Age. He discussed it with bassist Louis Vola, who began to scout around for players.

Vola heard about the Reinhardts and sat in with them. He sat in every night for three weeks. Vola had never played jazz quite like this before. Django played so fast, so far out, he could find harmonies Vola had never before found. His guitar could wheeze, sneeze, sing and cry – it could complain, exclaim, explain. Most of all explain. The meaning of life suddenly became clear to Vola. It was like religion, or a drug. Enlightenment. He wanted it all the time.

But Django was like sand; one day he blew away.

'Find him,' said Voltera, to whom Vola had spoken about Django. 'I want that Gypsy.'

Vola searched the bars, billiard parlours, Gypsy camps. Finally he found the Reinhardt caravan parked on a remote beach. But he was driving a borrowed car which resembled a police car from a distance. Django ran into the dunes to hide from it.

It was pure animal instinct. The police are just trouble for Gypsies; you do not have to be guilty of anything. They can always find a law you have broken. Scottish Gypsy slang for cop is 'balo', they've used it for centuries. *Balo* means pig.

Finally Vola pinned a 100-franc note to a piece of paper with his address on it, planted it in the sand and left.

Opening night at the Palm Beach Casino was a major event of the 1932 social season. Charlie Chaplin was there, Mistinguet, Maurice Chevalier. Vola did his Chevalier interpretation. He sang light-opera numbers, accompanying himself on accordion. It had nothing to do with the meaning of life, but a gig's a gig.

Django and Joseph had found Vola's note but neither could read it. There was no need to read the 100-franc note. Django had a new woman now. The two brothers and the woman decided to head south for sunny Italy. The road from Toulon to Italy passed through Cannes. Taking the air between sets one night, Vola spotted the Gypsies on the Croisette.

'Mister Vola,' said Django. 'How do you do?'

' "Mister"? You call me "mister" now?' For a Gypsy any *Gajo* who looks like he has money in his pocket is somehow automatically 'mister'. It had not been premeditated. Vola was one obvious 'mister' in his tuxedo.

After their three weeks of nightly musical brotherhood, Vola was insulted by the sudden distance. 'Where are you staying?' he asked, distant.

'The George V.'

Vola did not believe it, but a desk clerk had interpreted Django's silent impudence as the natural bearing of an Indian aristocrat. He counted on his woman to pay the bill: 'You can read palms on the Croisette.'

The woman began to cry. Vola took her in his arms. 'You've got to check out right away,' he said.

'OK.' Django was just as happy sleeping on the beach as in the Duke of Windsor's bed. He wanted what money could buy without having to worry about making it. The George V seemed to be becoming more trouble than it was worth.

The Reinhardts changed lodgings and Vola changed bands. It was now Louis Vola and His Brothers. Django rented a cabin on the beach near Théoule. There were apricot trees and rose bushes in the garden. He bought wine in fifty-litre casks. The butcher delivered entire animals. Gypsies and musicians were treated like visiting royalty.

The money burned. How much was left was not important. What it implied was important – success, acceptance. Django was like a child turned loose in a candy store, and like a child he was always testing his power. He issued Vola escalating ultimatums: 'I need a 5,000-franc advance. I want to buy my mother a bracelet. She deserves it, no? She has been a good mother to me. Five thousand or I don't play tonight.'

Vola advanced it. The next afternoon, Django drove up to the Casino in a 1926 Dodge. Having no driver's licence did not bother him in the least. What better throne for a twentieth-century prince than genuine leather seats? Nobody was allowed to handle the Dodge, not even mechanics. He never thought to check the oil or water levels. A car was supposed to move, that was all that mattered.

The exhaust pipe caught fire between Cannes and Golfe-Juan. Vola put it out with some sand. 'This car is worthless,' Django observed. He left the Dodge on the side of the road and never went back for it.

He used diminished, suspended and augmented chords way ahead of their time. He bought more cars. He could play any song in any key. He hosted more feasts. Django Reinhardt reinvented the guitar like Louis Armstrong reinvented the trumpet, and Joseph Goebbels was reinventing propaganda at just about the same time.

'Goebbels knew it was no longer possible to coerce the masses by states of emergency and nine o'clock curfews,' Helmut Heiber writes in his biography of Joseph Goebbels. German citizens were being graded continually and the root of the coercion was that they never learned the results of the tests. Indifference was not a fault in the system, it *was* the system. People began to suspect a wall was built around them, and then a real wall was built. The idea was to get the fear so deeply implanted that brainwashing would appear to be mere cosmetic compromise, coercion would no longer be needed. Heiber calls it 'voluntary compulsion'.

Voluntary compulsion.

White skin, a bald spot and grey temples help me duck behind cosmetic conformity. The idea is to trade surface for substance. Cops never stop little white cars. 'Hi there, officer, nice day isn't it?'

Marriage does not change anything. Written confirmation of a verbal commitment is redundant. Yet if marriage is meaningless why not get married? Society makes life easier when you are married to the person you're committed to. Cosmetic compromise.

At what depth did Michael Jackson caucasianize his features? Was it merely cosmetic? Voluntary? How about Polish Jews who anglicize their names?

Think of a father dedicated to profit, responsibilities and a secure retirement whose daughter decides to live with a jazz musician. Bob Dylan profiled the type: '. . . those who must obey authority they do not respect in any degree, who despise their jobs, their destiny, speak jealously of them that are free, cultivate their flowers to be nothing more than something they invest in'. What goes through the old man's mind? 'That slug-a-bed monkey sleeps until mid-afternoon and I have to get up at 7.30. He scratches himself and swings from trees every day, I only garden on weekends. Lovely ladies fall over him, I have to pay a whore. Interesting people in romantic places admire him, I'm just a schmucky tourist.' He drapes an arm over the young man's shoulder: 'Son, come into my business, you can always leave if you don't like it. I'll make you a partner. Blow your horn on weekends.'

Though fear of bureaucracy is central to their philosophy, totalitarian regimes want to appear reasonable to appeal to people of good will. People of good will are out-to-lunch. I know because I am one of them. Basically, we do not believe people of bad will exist, though they are all around us. Why should anyone want to hurt me? I'm so full of good will.

'We don't want to hurt you. We just want you to play good music.'

'How about the overture to *Tannhäuser*, sir?'

Voluntary compulsion.

'Nazi' stands for National Socialist and at the beginning it was a genuinely populist movement. Goebbels hated the bourgeoisie. As he attracted the masses, the Communists became competitors as well as ideological enemies. An ex-Catholic, he hated the church, the bourgeoisie and aristocrats too. He hated Jews of course. He hated.

He believed that revolutions are made by great communicators, not great writers or thinkers. (Ronald Reagan anticipated.) 'Information' was not designed to convey knowledge or to be fair or decent. Nazi posters consciously incorporated repulsive images. Anything at all, true or false, that would grab attention. Infiltration was the only aim. Propaganda need not be moral, truthful or beautiful; it should work. ('The medium is the message.') Goebbels said: 'Let them curse us, libel us, battle and beat us up, but let them talk about us.'

Eugene Hadamovsky, director of German State Radio, described him: 'In his unique personality, the religious impatience of a prophet was combined with the superior spirituality and reticent calm of an artist.'

'Christ never tried to prove the sermon on the mount,' Goebbels said.

The average age of employees in his Reich Ministry for Popular Enlightenment and Propaganda was younger than other ministries. Correspondence was written in eighties-style Madison Avenue shorthand: lively, short sentences. Goebbels cultivated a modern, youthful image. His telephone was an elaborate console with coloured buttons. In 1938 he wrote a memo: 'The minister (*sic!*) does not want to be addressed either verbally or in writing in the third person.'

The goal of propaganda was to: 'hammer party doctrine into the members so that they can repeat it in their sleep. We are simple because the people are simple. Our thoughts are primitive because the people think primitively. Earlier states controlled individuals, the Reich encompasses them.'

If a newspaper editor dealt with a subject Goebbels considered improper or not in line, he sent the SS to trash the paper. 'Journalists are too boring and try too hard to be accurate,' he said. The editor responsible for a sports writer who described a football match between Germans and Austrians, implying a distinction when the official line was that they were all Germans, was removed from the profession.

The writer was considered a 'literary soldier'. Hans Johst, president of the Reich Theatre Chamber, once joked that whenever somebody mentioned culture it made him want to reach for his revolver.

The Reich Radio Association installed loudspeaker pillars on street corners. Radios were mass-produced, their price reduced until miniature receivers cost thirty-five marks, the cheapest in the world. 'Community reception' was encouraged to bring in new listeners and to take the old ones out of the isolation of their homes, where they might think for themselves.

'It is foolish to believe that the regime can best be served by broadcasting crashing marches day after day,' he said. 'Ideological conviction need not imply boredom. Imagination must be used to bring ideology to the masses. It must be modern, relevant, interesting.'

He stressed 'cultural heritage': Beethoven cycles, Schiller, Bach, Mozart, Bruckner. Inaugurating 'Project Light-heartedness', he said: 'The majority of those who listen to the radio have been roughly treated by life ... they have a right to genuine relaxation and recreation in their leisure hours. For the conduct of war we need people in good spirits.'

In Nazi films, the postman said 'Good day', never '*Heil* Hitler' (voluntary compulsion). Artists who stayed in Germany enjoyed perks: social security, old-age pensions, paid vacations, rest homes. There were gifts, prizes and titles ('National Dramatic Artist'). Sometimes people would try too hard to please and even good Nazis laughed at 'Nazi kitsch'.

About jazz, he said: 'Now I shall speak quite openly on the question of whether German radio should broadcast so-called jazz music. If by jazz we mean music that is based on rhythm and entirely ignores or even shows contempt for melody, music in which rhythm is indicated primarily by the ugly sounds of whining instruments insulting to the soul, why then we can only reply to the question entirely in the negative.'

Before 1933 the line was against 'alien nigger music from the Hottentots'. Tangos and foxtrots were banned in favour of waltzes and marches. Music composed by a Negro or Jew was automatically banned. If the same sort of piece were written by an Aryan it might be allowed. Sometimes the name was simply not disclosed. March music reached epidemic proportions.

An appeal for clemency regarding a composer condemned to death for 'defeatist utterances' was denied. The judge said: 'He'd lose his head even if he was Beethoven.'

'This exceptional child is above schools and styles. If he had been sent to a conservatory, he might have become the J.S. Bach of our time.'

Georges Auric

Django Reinhardt decided to go to Paris to play with better musicians in more exposed situations. Saxophonist André Ekyan told Charles Delaunay about the first time he saw him: 'I didn't know who he was. He was just someone who had come to the club to hear us. But I noticed him right away, he struck me as outrageously antipathetic. I did not like the way he looked at me with those big, black, shiny absolutely expressionless eyes. He wasn't concerned with the impression he made on people.

'But I was with him at a jam session at the Swing Time club, on rue Fromentin. Benny Carter, Coleman Hawkins and Bill Coleman were also there. We began to play "I Won't Dance", a tune that modulates a lot as it is. We tried having fun playing it in odd keys. Bill Coleman gave up first, then Coleman Hawkins. Finally it was just Benny Carter and Django. Two masters.'

One night in 1934, the violinist Stephane Grappelli and Django Reinhardt were working a dance together in Louis Vola's fourteen-piece orchestra at the Claridge Hotel. They had met but were not friends. Grappelli broke a string, went to change it and came back tuning up with 'Dinah'. This is a famous story, historic folklore. Django joined in. They had both started playing music on the streets. Like Dave Brubeck with Paul Desmond and Charlie Parker with Dizzy Gillespie, the two of them were, for all their differences, made to improvise music together. That was about all they shared. Grappelli was personally about as different from Django Reinhardt as possible.

Together they formed the Quintet of the Hot Club de France, with Vola on bass and Joseph's rhythm guitar. They were idolized by violinists and guitarists everywhere; soon every European country had a drumless string band along the lines of their quintet, which also had a profound effect on the Afro-Americans who inspired it. It was the four of them until Django complained to Grappelli: 'It's not fair. You have two guitars backing you up. I only have one.'

A third guitar was added. This was one odd jazz band, without a saxophone, trumpet or drums. Grappelli has since called it 'the first rock 'n' roll band. I don't know anybody else who had three guitars before us.' The gay and swinging chamber sound of this string quintet was in fact the first European contribution to America's native art form.

On 3 September 1939, the quintet was in London. At 7.30 p.m. there was an air-raid alert. Thousands of civil-defence workers wearing white helmets patrolled the streets, blowing whistles and directing pedestrians to shelter. The streets were soon empty except for security people and their equipment. Searchlights probed the sky.

'It's war,' Django said to Grappelli.

That night at the State Kilburn Theatre, one Gypsy was missing. They looked for Django for days. Scotland Yard was put on the case. But he had taken a train for Paris after the first siren. Eating a *choucroute* in a Montmartre brasserie, Django explained to a friend: 'You're less afraid at home.'

13
The Bottomless Bottom

I hesitated before this chapter, but finally decided to go ahead with it. First there was this statement by Lowell Weicker, Senator from Connecticut: 'Apartheid exists because a whole world tolerates it by silence. The silence that envelops today's black South African is no different than that which wasted yesterday's European Jew.'

And then today, a report of a televised debate between South African prime minister R.F. Botha and Bishop Desmond Tutu, who compared apartheid with Nazism. Botha replied, angrily: 'To compare us with the Nazis is an insult to the more than 100,000 South Africans of Jewish origin who came to this country, and to our forefathers who fought with the Allied powers against Nazi Germany.'

Obviously South Africa is relevant.

Tying this particular past to the present is to take the subject out of dead history into contemporary adventure, from fact to faction, from the reference library to the battlefield. The opportunity to compare two of the most racist regimes in history can be considered a break. The present clarifies the past.

When I was offered a three-and-a-half-week tour of Africa by the United States Information Service, I hesitated before accepting because one of the countries would be South Africa. I was aware of the UN-sponsored cultural boycott but, checking around, I was told that because we would be sponsored by the US government, not a local promoter, and because we would be a racially-integrated group playing for racially-integrated audiences, we should be exempt. Later in the tour, in Lesotho, we ran into Hugh Masekela, one of South Africa's most famous musical emigrés, and an old friend from New York. He confirmed it (I have it on tape).

In any case the boycott laws provide for atonement by writing and/or speaking about the truth of this evil system, the most evil system since Nazi Germany, which I am doing.

First I asked the band – Oliver Johnson, drums; Jack Gregg, bass; and John Thomas, guitar – if they were willing. (Oliver and John are black, Jack and I white. Sorry to segregate us by race, even parenthetically, but race is everything in South Africa; the entire system is built on race as it was in Nazi Germany. You are forced to think in racial terms. Equal racial pairing had been the only solution. A white leader with a black rhythm section would have been back to the plantation, while only one black could be seen as tokenism. So two and two it would be.)

We were curious to see for ourselves, we did not like other people telling us what to do. We agreed we would refuse to play in a so-called homeland but frankly none of us was anxious to turn down a well-paid jazz job.

Welcome aboard South African Airways, a plentiful vehicle. It looks like all first-class, divided into cosy, padded sections with wide seats and stretched leg room, unlimited free alcoholic beverages, sleeping slippers and masks, digestible food, and the hi-fi earphones (no mere plugs) are free. This is the national flag-carrier of a leper state. Discounting the risk of contagion, you will never be more comfortable in the air. South Africa sells gold, diamonds, uranium and exports food; it is a developed economy, a lucrative market, anybody with hard money is welcome. Black or white. But look at their route map. Red lines from Europe swing west over the Atlantic because no African state will admit to allowing SAA to overfly their territory. However, just about every black and Socialist African nation does business with South Africa, the richest country on their continent, and SAA flies to many of them, boycotts and route maps notwithstanding. Other national flag-carriers also fly here, so boycotting SAA is one easy decision; appease your conscience and get there anyway. Thus the over-design, and the (all-white) crew wearing nice-people masks.

'The whole system is based on "now you see it now you don't. It's there; it's not there." They sure know how to tap dance.'

Hugh Masekela

When a stewardess, indifferent to the fact that I am sitting next to a black man who is obviously my friend, asks if I want black or white coffee, I answer 'black' even though I would have preferred cream.

The in-flight magazine, *Flying Springbok*, lists a jazz audio track including 'Cape Town Fringe' by Dollar Brand, 'Caution' by Hugh Masekela, and Abbey Lincoln's 'Africa'. How bad can this country really be if they present music by two of their political exiles and one black-power militant on their national flag-carrier? But when I switch on the so-called jazz channel, I find only the Carpenters. The jazz is listed but it is not there. This is a good example of what Afrikaners call 'progress' and Africans call 'cosmetic bullshit'.

It's there; it's not there.

To express what they considered fascist tendencies in their country, 1960s' flower children derogated the name 'Amerika'. The hard German 'k' implied Nazism, blitzkriegs, and Ku Klux Klan. The name of the tribe of Dutch ancestry that presides over South Africa has the 'k' organically. Called Afrikaners, these people speak Afrikaans, in which language their country is written 'Suid Afrika'. Afrikaners descend from Boers, which sounds like boor, bore and of course boar, an ugly and vicious animal. Another white tribe, of English descent ('good Germans'), generally disapproves of the Afrikaner National Party in power and its policy of racial separation called apartheid, though they are powerless to stop it in a police state and they profit from it all the same. In the broad English South African accent the first word of their country's name is pronounced between 'Suid' and 'South', something like 'Sad'. So we will refer to it as 'Sad Afrika'.

The Sad Afrikan system can be described by parodying Winston Churchill ... *Never have so few with so much given so little to so many.*

When I called a journalist whose name had been given me by a friend, he said: 'Welcome to Hateland.' Based on hate, fear, bigotry and greed, hypocritically justified in biblical terms, Sad Afrika has turned itself into an extraordinarily violent society with suicide, divorce, road-accident, alcoholism and crime rates among the highest in the world. Masekela can hardly be accused of hyperbole when he describes the place as a 'slave pit'.

'The best lack all conviction, The worst are full of passionate intensity.'

William Butler Yeats

Oliver Johnson had been told in our briefing: 'You will be considered an honorary white while you are there.' He laughed: 'I've been a nigger in Oakland and New York and Paris all my life. I have to go to Joburg to be white?' One reason Oliver was ready and even eager to go to Sad Afrika was because, 'There's a lady down in Joburg I would really like to see again.' Behind Oliver's quintessentially cool hipster exterior lies a lively intelligence and warm sensitivity; his motivation should not imply shallowness. One thing I like about jazz musicians is their ability to cut through political and structural abstractions and take life on a truly humanistic level. It is one reason they were considered so dangerous by the Nazis. After reading an article in the *Rand Daily Mail* about Sidney Poitier calling for a stricter cultural boycott, Oliver said: 'Sidney's straight. He's got his big house in LA. He can afford to turn down a gig.'

When we arrived at Jan Smuts airport, we found reporters and photographers scrambling to get to us. 'That's my picture,' a dark-skinned photographer shouted at a white competitor, who backed off. His photo appeared large and in colour on the front page of the *Rand Daily Mail* the following day. There we were, two blacks and two whites smiling together. How bad can apartheid be if a black photographer can successfully compete with a white one to take the picture of two blacks and two whites who are allowed to travel around playing music together for multi-racial audiences, stay at the same hotels and eat in the same restaurants?

Now you see it; now you don't.

Expensive international hotels and the restaurants in them are free-fire zones. Come in with a green woman, nobody looks twice.

They sure know how to tap dance.

The papers were full of a story about an Afrikaner farmer on trial for murdering his wife with an axe who was also accused of having an affair with a black woman. The prosecution offered to bargain: plead guilty to the lesser charge and get a lighter sentence on the murder. But Detective Warrant Officer Martin Van Niekerk 'told the court he thought the farmer considered the allegation that he had a relationship with a black woman worse than the murder charge'.

'There are more crooked businessmen per square metre in Johannesburg than there are anyplace else in the world.'
Flying Springbok magazine

A reporter from the *Johannesburg Star* asked Oliver about the boycott, and he answered (it was printed): 'We are here to try and create something positive. Music has been used in Africa for many things, from circumcision onwards – there is music for everything. Albert Ayler once said, "Music is the healing force", and perhaps we can heal some negative things. I don't know, but we can have a shot. We've nothing to lose.'

Nothing to lose. Just our careers. Serious people are behind the cultural boycott and there is no way anyone with the slightest moral scruple could argue with the boycott's aims. The means, perhaps. You might argue with the means.

First ask who's being boycotted. A band I once had played a small Parisian festival. My drummer, who was on the same bill later on with his own group, had a disagreement with the promoter and, just before we were to go on, he screamed: 'If I don't get paid right now, I'm not playing.' I said to him: 'Wait a minute, man, you're aiming at him but you're shooting *me* down.' If you aim at the bank robber and hit the hostage, or miss the master and hit the slave, that is not exactly the point.

When I told him I was going, Claude Verses asked me, furious, 'Would you have gone to play in Nazi Germany?' Good question. It stumped me for a while, but it depends who I would have played with and for. I would have gone with other Jews to play in stalags, concentration camps and ghettos. Sad Afrika is the closest system we have to Nazi Germany. Not to say they are unique in political repression or racial discrimination. But it is the only system today built on racial discrimination; it *is* the system. And, as in Nazi Germany, prosperity is based on what amounts to slave labour.

The black township of Soweto lies some twelve miles from Joburg, as Johannesburg is familiarly known (though to use such a jaunty name for such a slave pit is actually in questionable taste).

We played two concerts at Soweto's Orlando YMCA. Local musicians sat in after the second one, including an extraordinary saxophone player named Winston 'Mankuku' Ngozi, who has a style somewhere between Joe Henderson and Albert Ayler. Later, one of the musicians said: 'Send us the big shots. Send us Art Blakey and Elvin Jones. We know them. We have their records. We will pay them ourselves. We are paid slave wages by this shit government but we will find the money somehow. We don't have cars, we don't even have bicycles. We don't have street lights. When we leave here tonight, everybody walks home in the dark. When I heard you guys the first night, I didn't dream we would play together. But you have given us some inspiration. It's great to play with Americans. When Americans play jazz, it's the real thing. Now we want to form a group. I don't think you should boycott *us*.'

In *Looking on Darkness*, the dissident Afrikaner writer André Brink described Soweto:

> ... with its phalanxes of identical houses, row upon row like the crosses of Delville Wood, with bare patches of bleeding red earth in between, erosion ditches, water taps, the stench of bad sanitation ... groups of teenagers in smart clothes or in rags, yelling at the passing women, occasionally grabbing one, children playing noisily with stones and wheels and broken dolls, children fighting, children pissing in the street. Cars parked ... enormous black American monsters from ten years ago, old wrecks with wide-open doors like chickens nestling in the sun ... Street lamps protected by wire mesh; a white goat, women breast-feeding their babies in front of their houses, a child beaten barbarously with a leather thong; and far away, far but visible, a barbed-wire fence to hedge it all in, to stop the march of those regiments of houses ... The muddy mess of early morning, half-past four, five o'clock, six, when the people go to work in the rain; the sound of thousands of feet, the low hum of voices ... children crying. Children crying at night ... sudden outbursts of sounds, shouts. Silence – the low ominous drone of police vans passing in the streets, patrols on prescribed hours, two o'clock and all's hell ... Always the police were near;

everywhere I was accompanied by the laugh of Harry Tsabalala. 'What else can you expect? There's more than a million of us here, man, and we've got nothing to keep us busy; but we're not doing too badly, d'you think? We fuck and murder and dance and die, never a dull moment . . .'

'All non-Bantu entering this area must have permission, and may not spend the night.'

sign near Soweto

The sale of skin-lightener is illegal. Though the weather is magnificent and there are miles and miles of empty beaches, you don't see many white people with deep suntans in Sad Afrika.

Never before have I been to a place where, when a native asks you how you like his or her country, you are morally obliged to answer in the negative. Usually you can find something good to say about any place. When Sad Afrikans defend themselves: 'But it's beautiful, isn't it?' you must answer: 'No it isn't.' You cannot separate the glorious mountains, green valleys, temperate climate and gleaming cities from what takes place there.

There are many whites, including Afrikaners, of good will in Sad Afrika, but people of good will are, as I have said, out-to-lunch, and the National Party in power acts as though it is on a wagon train drawn into a circle surrounded by screaming savages. The problem is tribal more than racial, only here the tribes that have all the marbles, which are numerous and sparkle, are white. (It should be remembered that both white tribes have been in Sad Afrika for hundreds of years and so have a right to be called natives.) They are outnumbered, paranoid; they believe the rest of the world does not understand them. They are prepared to survive without the rest of the world if necessary. They have developed their sort of 'final solution' to take care of the Africans, whom they believe to be an inferior race. Even reactionaries in other countries are forced (publicly at least) to call them outlaws. They do feel like outlaws. They *are* outlaws – lepers.

Afrikaners are big-boned strong people who feel called on to work the land. They worked hard and the land works, though they do not let any other race own the land. With the growth of mechanized farming, Afrikaner youth is migrating to urban areas and it is said that they are more liberal than their parents. But any Afrikaner who takes a stand against apartheid is considered a traitor.

'Tour of Soweto, eighteen Rand ($16).'
                                      sign in Joburg Holiday Inn

To understand Sad Afrika it is essential to deal with the 'so-called' qualification. A republic that does not give the vote to more than eighty-five per cent of its population (seventy-five per cent black, ten per cent coloured and Asian) and denies them the most basic civil rights is certainly a so-called republic. Blacks have recently been granted their so-called freedom in the form of so-called homelands – tracts of badlands comparable to American Indian reservations – where they are now citizens and where there is just about no employment, water or food. (No country but Sad Afrika has recognized any homeland as a so-called sovereign state.) They are granted visas to work or study in Sad Afrika, their own country.

Omitting the so-called qualification implies acceptance of the basic principles of apartheid. White people of good will and all people of darker hues drop about one 'so-called' a minute.

In Joburg, John Thomas bought a bush jacket and a wide-brimmed khaki hat with leopard-skin band. He wore one side snapped up against the crown. He wore it on stage. 'A black man doesn't wear a *b'wana* hat in this country,' said an embarrassed USIS official. 'Doesn't he realize the symbolism?' Oliver took to calling him 'Jungle John'. The USIS official asked me to ask John not to wear his *b'wana* hat on stage. When we played the University of Zululand, segregated black, a professor asked John, forcing a laugh: 'Going into the bush?' But no way was I going to talk to John about his hat. It was just a hat, after all, kind of ugly, but only a hat. Why can't a black man wear a *b'wana* hat if he feels like it? It could have been a political statement on his part, and if so I agreed with it. Asking him not to wear it would have omitted the 'so-called'.

We played the black townships of Mamelodi, near Pretoria and Soweto, near Joburg. Our audiences were never exclusively white. Sometimes all-black but never all-white. We gave workshops for black students on days off. We harboured guilt; what were nice guys like us doing in a place like this? We felt the need to leave something, to give something. Perhaps one answer to the cultural boycott question is to levy a sort of tax, a percentage of the artist's earnings to be paid to black township charities. But Ford, Apple, Colonel Sanders, Boeing, Holiday Inn and a long list of other companies do business in Sad Afrika. The columns of Art Buchwald and Russell Baker are syndicated there, American banks operate there, Hertz and Avis rent cars there. An item in a liberal magazine criticizing Linda Ronstadt for performing in Sad Afrika was separated by a few pages from an ad for De Beers diamonds. Why should musicians be the only ones to turn down Sad Afrikan money?

A total boycott on all levels would certainly bring down the regime. There is no doubt they should be treated like the lepers they are. But this is unlikely so long as they have all that cash. And in the meantime it seemed and still seems to me that the mere presence of two whites and two blacks on stage making music together, hanging out together afterwards, even arguing with each other, is a positive political statement.

The University of South Africa, UNISA, on a hill overlooking Pretoria, is multi-racial and billed as the largest correspondence school in the world. It has a sprawling modern plant and you might be impressed, until you realize that a multi-racial correspondence school, where students rarely see each other, is a farce in a segregated society.

After a noonday concert there, we were taken upstairs for lunch in the penthouse dining-room. A student choir from Windhoek, Namibia (South-west Africa) sang for us on the sun-drenched terrace. Namibia is still under Sad Afrikan trusteeship dating from the League of Nations after World War I, despite heavy pressure from the UN to grant independence. The choir consisted of seventeen teenagers, all shades of brown and black plus one pale German girl who can 'click away like a native' according to their white director. (Some tribal languages use clicks for 'Q' and other letters.) The youngsters looked clean and happy to be together. They sang in tune. They had good time and ears. The director, a prematurely bald young man with a bright face – no doubt of good will – said: 'They represent ten ethnic groups and twenty languages.' They sang ethnic songs with gusto. If such a racially mixed group of apparently happy and healthy children can tour Sad Afrika (sponsored by the Dutch Reform Church) how bad can it be?

Now let's go through the looking-glass and into another perspective on Namibia. From the *Zimbabwe Chronicle* (not distributed in Sad Afrika; I found it later in Botswana):

> South Africa has stationed more than 100,000 troops in this mineral-rich country. . . Blacks do not have access to hospitals and are dying largely of diseases against which they could be immunized . . . Windhoek medic, Dr Kenneth Abrahams, leader of the Namibian Independence Party, said he wouldn't be surprised if the social misery is part of a deliberate plan to demoralize blacks . . . A Roman Catholic priest, the Rev Klein-Hitpas, said children between eleven and thirteen detained for stealing clothes told him policemen had administered electric shocks through their fingers and ears.

So much for good ears.

'In terms of the city's bylaws it is legal for members of any race to use the beaches but only members of the specific race group for which the beach is zoned may enter the water or swim.'

> Durban daily paper

Three weeks in Sad Afrika is like having a protracted disease: at first you wish for good health, then you forget what good health is.

'One and a half million people live in Soweto; it is the biggest city in this country and the name is not even written on the map.'

> Hamilton of Soweto

Hamilton of Soweto sells insurance during the day. He listens to some of his 3,000 jazz records at night. When he can get a gig he plays the saxophone. Actually, he does not sell insurance, he may live somewhere else and perhaps he plays some other instrument. He asked me to disguise him because, 'They'd blow me sky-high for the things I'm telling you. They'd rough me up. They've roughed me up before.'

He looks for contributions to purchase music and art supplies for workshops to keep black township youth occupied. He had been talking about art not politics and when I asked him why he was afraid of being identified, he answered: 'If you're positive, you're dangerous. If you're effective on any level, you're dangerous. In other words, it's dangerous if you don't wear a mask. You leave the ghetto and go into the city and as you travel out of here and into the white suburbs of the city, you should not be aware of the beauty that surrounds you, even though you helped create it.'

White residential areas are luxurious: square miles of rambling houses, manicured gardens, lush trees, swimming-pools behind painted walls. Sometimes chain-link walls. There are articles in the papers arguing the relative merits of protective walls. Always everywhere walls.

Only whites can live in the cities that are on the map and their suburbs, though you see mostly blacks on the streets. Every white household has at least one black servant. Whites ride in Mercedes, blacks ride buses or walk. If you are black you live, say, twelve miles from the city; classified so-called coloured, you might get seven miles closer; Indians have paved streets. The system is a highly evolved, self-righteous, computerized, pitiless, dogmatic, tribal internal colonialism. It is structured to stifle the ingenuity and initiative of the majority and keep it subservient and cheap. Its defenders build walls around their houses and live in fear. The system involved a great deal of cleverness to construct and requires constant attention and ingenuity to enforce. Each layer connects to the other with diabolical consistency. It is probably too elaborate to unglue. It has to explode. The fuse is lit. The fire is approaching the magazine. It's the *Lusitania*, the *Hindenburg*. Pardner, it's time to get out of Dodge City.

Hamilton (which may not be his name) continued: 'So you wear a mask until you get to work at 8 a.m. and all of a sudden you're expected to be intelligent, observant, creative and positive – until you stop working and go back home, and then you have to put on the same mask again. You come back like nothing happened, as though you had not gone through the looking-glass. You should smile all the time and say everything is just fine. That's it. As soon as you move in a direction where you try to improve the situation, you are dangerous.

'Look, we want to create a positive black mind, to say, "Here I am in the swamp but I'm going to drain that swamp." The people who run this country want it to remain a swamp. It keeps our minds in check. Goodness me, it's brain cancer, like Hitler's Germany.

'Only this is a concentration camp of the mind. If you're too intelligent you get crazy. As soon as you start serious thinking you are in serious trouble. You really do begin believing that ignorance is bliss after a while. It's like Orwell; check out Orwell.'

The parallel between the Proles in Orwell's *Nineteen Eighty-four* and black Sad Afrikans in 1984 is astounding. They are both majorities herded into ghettos and treated as subhuman, and any hope for a positive future of both societies rests with them.

'You know how I stay sane here?' Hamilton concluded: 'Music. Without it, I'd sink into a bottomless bottom. Right. That's it. There are emotions that words cannot express. I stay sane by screaming into a saxophone.'

■Otto Jung (bass), Carlo Bohlander (centre) and Horst Lippmann (left) with friends, Frankfurt, 1944

■Carlo Bohlander (trumpet), Otto Jung (piano) and Horst Lippmann (bass) with friends, Frankfurt, 1944

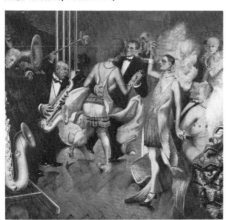

■Grosstadt (Triptychon), Otto Dix, 1928

■Otto Jung, Frankfurt, 1944

■Dietrich Schulz-Koehn, 1980

■Carlo Bohlander (seated) under 100lbs

■Carlo Bohlander (left) and (right) Charly Petri, on leave from the army, with 'Black Charlie' (real name Friedel Borlinghaus). 'He was no musician but we wanted him in the picture as a kind of symbol of jazz, and also to document our anti-racist attitude'

■George Scott's jazz band

■George Scott, July 1943

■George Scott conducting at a contest between a
jazz band and a symphony orchestra, Warsaw,
June 1943

■Bronislaw Stasiak's jazz band, Cafe Club, 1940

■The Golden Seven

■The elegant Adria restaurant, Warsaw 1940

■Delaunay drawing Django, 1942

■Hugues Panassié in Montauban

■Django Reinhardt at fourteen

■Django at eighteen

■Django and Stephane Grappelli, Stockholm, 1939

■(Left to right): Joseph Reinhardt, Django, Pierre Fouad, Francis Luca and Josette Daydé, ABC, 1940

■Edith Piaf reading Django Reinhardt's palm

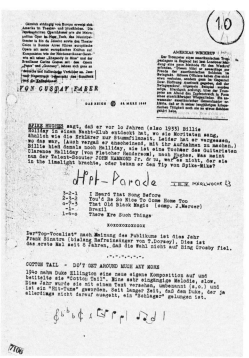

■ Contemporary clandestine newsletter

■ Svend Asmussen, 1984

■ Charles Delaunay (left), Django and Pierre Fouad (right), 1942

14
Out of the Game

Closing the door of his small office in an obscure corner of a remote wing of the Vogue Records building, which he owns, to keep out the noise of Abba and Bo Diddley, Charles Delaunay admits: 'I'm no longer in the game.'

Delaunay is still listed on the masthead of *Jazz Hot* magazine, but it's in name only, out of respect for the past and to help with banks and printers. Since he started it in 1935, jazz has gone from hot to swing to cool to modal to free to fusion and funk. *Jazz Hot* has become more sound than meaning, and the youngblood editors who took the magazine past its fiftieth anniversary have expanded the definition to include just about anything that moves.

Delaunay lost his faith when jazz stopped being hot. He considers modern congregations heretical, blasphemous, money-changers in the temple. Although he made a fortune on the devil's music, he has not corrupted the holy men. He changed his money in the bank, where money belongs. Today's musical Tower of Babel is not what he sold his meticulously accumulated stamp collection for when the fledgling magazine could not pay its bills.

The Schism with Panassié, in 1947, was caused by the arrival of 'Salt Peanuts', a record with a red label. Hot Club members took pride in being the first Frenchmen to hear new American jazz recordings, and members formed a line up the stairs to Delaunay's second-floor office in the club pavilion in a courtyard on rue Chaptal to hear Charlie Parker and Dizzy Gillespie.

'Everybody was amazed,' Delaunay recalls. He paused and you could sense him thinking that if only they had known what heresies bebop would spawn they might not have been so welcoming: 'I wrote Panassié and said, "You have to hear this. It's a revolution." He wrote back, "I absolutely must have that record." Panassié always had to be first to discover something or somebody and since he did not discover bebop, he was automatically against it.'

After Delaunay and Panassié severed connections, other revolutions followed; Delaunay severed connections of his own. He formed the Vogue record company in 1948. Sidney Bechet's 'Les Ognons', a jazz version of a New Orleans creole folk song, sold a million copies. Now a multi-million-dollar enterprise, Vogue has been called the 'house that Bechet built'.

After Bechet followed with another hit, 'Petite Fleur', the company began to suffer from success in the form of high overheads and inadequate cash flow and turned to the 'yeh-yeh' music of Françoise Hardy and Johnny Hallyday in the sixties, which made big francs. Gradually Delaunay lost interest in Vogue as he had lost interest in the direction of the music he loved. He was left with the money and the past.

He holds his cards close to his vest; you don't really know how he feels about you or about life. He appears to be waiting for the next mistake, one more misstep, to confirm his worst suspicions. He is not waiting for the sunrise.

Delaunay's mother and father, Sonia and Robert, were famous painters, at the centre of French cultural life during their prime. Diaghilev, Stravinsky and Nijinsky were frequent house guests. His parents did not so much disapprove of young Charles as not take him seriously. Looking to find something of his own, he collected stamps and listened to jazz, promoted jazz, then had to sell his stamp collection to feed jazz. His taste and energy dominated French jazz as thoroughly as John Hammond in the US (although Hammond continued to play long after Delaunay left the game). Delaunay was paid little or nothing at all; the Hot Club was his mistress, not a whore. So when jazz ran off with younger men, it was a bitter separation. How could she have deserted him after all he did for her? He is a man who has been hurt and at seventy-five years of age he appears to have built heavy psychic security systems to make sure it won't happen again.

Delaunay keeps his distance from contemporary games in his remote corner of the Vogue building in Villetaneuse, a working-class suburb of Paris. He gets up at five in the morning in his comfortable home in exclusive Chantilly to work on his memoirs, writing by hand, and goes to his office by ten to type it up. Late mornings in the office mean at least one thing to do today. And Vogue distributes his small reissue label, Nec Plus Ultra, which includes a recording of the Dizzy Gillespie big band live in Paris in 1953, just about when Charles Delaunay lost his faith.

On 21 February 1935, the first issue of the world's first jazz magazine was not exactly launched like *Vanity Fair*. The printer had declared bankruptcy. Combination editor, art director, reporter, columnist, advertising manager, proofreader and distributor, Delaunay spent all night in the printing plant giving birth without a doctor's help. It was not painless.

The first editorial announced, '*Jazz Hot* is the only review entirely consecrated to real jazz music.' The first 'issue' was one page printed on the back of a programme for a concert by Coleman Hawkins at Salle Pleyel. The copies arrived during intermission.

Down Beat magazine had been founded four months earlier and *Melody Maker* already existed, but they were general-interest publications and when they covered jazz at all it was the pale variety of Paul Whiteman or the Casa Loma Orchestra. Delaunay felt that bad Duke Ellington was better than good Glenn Miller; the 'real thing' was coming from Louis Armstrong, Ellington and other black geniuses who were still considered monkeys by white American entertainment moguls.

If the magazine needed some cash, musicians would empty their pockets. Fifteen francs here, ten there. They were proud to be 'marginal', 'underground'. Solidarity was palpable, faith solid. The air was full of joyous prayer, not fear of the future and failure; false gods did not then reign.

Every evening before work, the musicians all sat in the same cafe on rue Fontaine. The Hot Club offices were around the corner. The gigs were all nearby in Montmartre; you could find the musicians drinking an aperitif on rue Fontaine before taking off for Chez Florence, El Garonne, Music Box, La Cabane Cubaine. Delaunay forgets the name of the cafe; it's called something else now.

Chez Florence was for snobs – the Prince of Wales, the count of this, the duchess of that. The *maître d'* at the door knew who counted – he often banned Delaunay for being poor and in the company of dark-hued people. The orchestra was always black; Afro-American jazzmen were chic in Paris that season. They played from when the first customer arrived until the last one left. After work they went to the Music Box to jam with Big Boy Goody. During the occupation, most of those joints catered to Germans, who had the money. Champagne as usual. The Afro-Americans went home.

There was always a table reserved for musicians in Chez Berthe, right across the street from the Hot Club on rue Chaptal. Everybody would meet for lunch Chez Berthe. Sometimes Django Reinhardt would come in wearing pyjamas and slippers. But the offices of *Jazz Hot* have moved to the Champs Elysées and Chez Berthe is called something else, too.

15
I Just Made It Up

By the summer of 1939 the Germans were infiltrating Danzig. War looked inevitable. Would Paris be bombed? Would the Germans use poison gas? Parisians ate *bouillabaisse* on sunny sidewalks. The German–Soviet treaty was signed, reactionaries had been right: the Soviet Union was just another imperialistic power serving selfish interests. John Ford's *Stagecoach* opened on the Champs Elysées.

Touring Holland, Django Reinhardt was surrounded backstage by a mob of fans seeking autographs. He could hardly write his own name; it took him hours to get out of there.

Some leftist intellectuals suspected that the men in the Kremlin were secretly pleased by the blitzkrieg in the west because it would aid the eventual victory of world Communism. Germany was short of bread, petrol, steel and everything else. Germany would be wiped out, the Reich would collapse. Hjalmar Schacht had said: 'You can end a war with bread rationing if absolutely unavoidable, but never start one in that condition.' Let Hitler finish what he started. '*Garçon, encore un verre de rouge.*'

Germany declared war on Poland in September. France was mobilized. In her book *The Prime of Life*, Simone de Beauvoir remarks on the 'beautiful moon hanging over Saint Germain des Pres' that month. Cafes closed at eleven and the nightclubs were not open at all. People lined up for gas masks.

The Quintet of the Hot Club of France changed bassists. Django Reinhardt hired somebody who did not please the others. 'We can do better than that,' his brother Joseph complained. Django agreed that maybe he did not play so well, but on the road you spend fourteen hours travelling, eating and hanging out and only two hours playing music and if he wasn't the best bass player in the world, he smiled all the time, was a good storyteller and he played one hell of a game of billards.

The police wore new tin helmets and carried gas masks in little brown satchels. Several metro stations were shut and barricaded. Vehicle headlights were painted blackout blue. A policeman argued with the manager of the Dome Cafe about escaping light and finally a thick blue curtain was hung over that window. Buses were camouflaged.

Django liked to lounge around his hotel room, ringing for room service or maids. Their horror at finding him half-naked in bed amused him. He left for a tour without his passport. 'I'm famous,' he said. 'I don't need a passport.' He was shipped back on the next train.

France declared war. The first air-raid sirens went off in the middle of the night. It was a false alarm. A man on a bicycle shook a fist and shouted 'the bastards'. Two women in floppy housecoats wore underwear wrapped around their faces as make-do gas masks.

Django was working in Hot Feet, a tiny club on rue Notre-Dame de Lorette. At 2 a.m. an imposing black man caused a sensation when he sat down at a table. The Gypsy was too busy playing to notice it was Duke Ellington. Finally they exchanged smiles; Ellington sat down at the piano and they played together. Django shook his head from side to side for a few beats, sighing: 'Ah, my friend.'

A decree ordered all Germans residing in France to be put in prison camps. A sign in a Uniprix shop read: 'French firm, French directors, French capital'. Foreign residents had to register with the police, many started leaving. Telegrams begin to arrive: 'Your husband has fallen honourably on the field of battle . . . We are sorry to inform you . . .' Women worried waiting for mail.

Django introduced a Louis Vola bass solo: 'Monsieur Solo will now take a Vola.'

Crossword puzzles were banned for fear of their being used as codes. Cafes demanded COD, just in case the roof suddenly caved in. Warsaw fell.

The door of the dressing-room in the Moulin Rouge was full of holes after Django Reinhardt and his cousins got through throwing knives into it between sets.

Rain held up the blitzkrieg for a while. There were rumours of severe restrictions inside Germany, and mounting resentment and discontent. Parisians could not quite believe it was really happening. There seemed to be a war somewhere.

Late one night, or rather early one morning, a weary unpressed and depressed Django Reinhardt walked into Le Boeuf sur le Toit. He had just lost 100,000 francs playing chemin de fer. 'Monsieur Moises,' his weak voice called the barman, 'champagne.' As Jo Bouillon's orchestra packed their instruments, he picked up a guitar on the bandstand and began strumming a little melody which would earn him hundreds of times the night's losses. Suffering is not for nothing. He called the little melody 'Nuages'.

Some French soldiers mutilated themselves to avoid the front. German propaganda posters appeared: 'We have nothing against the French; we won't shoot unless you do.' Over short-wave radio, a German mother told French mothers that the war was the fault of the English: 'Why should French men get killed to defend the Brits?'

The Quintet of the Hot Club de France crossed Germany by train on their way to tour Scandinavia. Nobody had thought about transit visas. They were taken off the train in Aachen. A peculiar lighting effect made the Führer's moustache on the painting on the wall of the customs office appear to quiver. Django looked at the Führer and laughed. He could not stop; it became a fit. Grappelli had to do some fancy talking to get out of that one. Across the water in Sweden, Django moped when the garland of flowers reserved for distinguished visitors was hung over Grappelli's neck.

Cars were breaking down everywhere. Travellers took trains carrying suitcases full of silverware to hide in grandma's house. Sirens alternated with deathly silence. House planking became a big business.

After living together for fifteen years, Django suddenly decided to marry his woman, Naguine.

Alsace had been bouncing between Germany and France for centuries, and though it was French for the moment, Alsatians, even French soldiers, began to brush up their rusty German. Germans and French soldiers waved to each other while fishing on opposite sides of the Rhine. When a German machine-gun suddenly went off, a sign went up: 'French soldiers, please forgive us, it was an accident – we don't want to shoot you.'

After an unsatisfactory answer to his question: 'Are you sure it's safe?' Django Reinhardt refused to be parachuted to the stage of the

Medrano Circus in a star-shaped gondola hanging from silver ribbons. It was his own idea; he had been elated with it: 'In Las Vegas Mae West arrives on stage like that,' he had said. 'Very American.'

In December, 1939, Pan American Airlines pilot Pete Clausen flew Torkild 'Cap' Rieber, a partner in Standard Oil of California, and Herman Goering on a tour of German industrial facilities. Rieber supplied oil to Franco during the Spanish civil war, transmitted polymerization techniques to IG Farben and sailed his tankers through the British blockade to fuel Nazi U-boats.

Drifts remained piled on Paris sidewalks after a snowstorm in February, 1940. The shovellers were in the army. Patisseries were closed three days a week. No alcohol was available on three 'dry days' a week. In early April, Hitler predicted that he would enter Paris before 15 June. He was not taken seriously in the Cafe Flore. Germany invaded Holland, Belgium and Luxembourg.

Django took a suite in the luxurious Claridge Hotel, then an apartment on rue des Acacias near the Arc de Triomphe. He worked in Le Doyen, a snazzy restaurant in the Champs Elysées gardens.

Seventy thousand French soldiers threw down their arms and ran for it. Frontiers were sealed. Paul Reynaud said on the radio: 'If I were told that only a miracle could save France, I would say I believe in miracles because I believe in France.' The Paris opera presented Darius Milhaud's *Médée*. The music struck Simone de Beauvoir as 'fine', and the overall presentation 'quite remarkable'.

Charles Delaunay wrote in *Jazz Hot*: 'We hope that our recent concerts and radio programmes have helped to overcome the absurd prejudice the French have against their own jazz talent. Our next issue will list our choice of the ten best records of the year.'

Paris was bombed on 4 June. Anti-aircraft guns shot little puffs of white smoke, as groups of people stood in cafes drinking and trying to figure out how not to be caught 'like a rat' in occupied Paris. Great streams of exodus traffic clogged the boulevards. Entire quarters were making a run for it. Taxis were assaulted rather than hailed. Trucks loaded with beds, bicycles and scared families were stuck in long stationary lines and people picnicked by the side of the road. Italy declared war.

A titled French lady threw frequent parties to which she invited people from opposing walks of life. One evening she asked both Andres Segovia and Django Reinhardt to perform. Segovia arrived on time and impressed the guests with his repertoire. Django came three hours late without a guitar. He was smiling, he thought everything was just fine. He never knew the time. He did not wear a watch. He went by the sun and the moon. Segovia refused to loan Django his guitar so someone rushed off and came back with an old box with a cracked bridge. Segovia was amazed at what sounds the old box could produce. 'Where can I get that music?' he asked. 'Nowhere,' Django laughed. 'I just made it up.'

On the morning of 17 June, from his Hotel du Parc headquarters in the *fin-de-siècle* watering hole of Vichy, Maréchal Philippe Pétain announced: 'It is with heavy heart that I tell you we must give up the struggle.' Pétain called out to youth for a 'crusade', an 'orderly national revolution', for 'moral and intellectual renewal. I count on our youth. I put all my heart and energy at its disposal.' Loudspeakers blared martial music.

Controllers lost track of trains. Clocks were set to German time. Grubby grumbling refugees made a startling contrast with the well-groomed, cheerful, courteous Germans. A sign in a shop window: 'Jews not welcome.' Ham disappeared from the butcher shops. Vichy radio denounced 'renegade Jews' who had 'deserted the homeland in time of need' by leaving for America. A Django Reinhardt record was worth two kilos of butter on the black market. Factories fired 'Jews and foreigners'. It was forbidden to applaud during newsreels.

Django hired a young unknown Algerian named Hubert Rostaing to play clarinet, replacing Stephane Grappelli in the new quintet. Rostaing was a saxophonist who had never played either jazz or the clarinet before. 'I like your volume,' Django told him. 'You're hired.'

'Place your confidence in the German soldier' posters appeared. A lecture by André Gide was cancelled by the authorities in Nice. The newspaper *Je Suis Partout* published frenzied editorials denouncing Communists, Jews and anti-fascist writers: 'We demand the right to expose the traitors in our midst.'

The English symbol 'V', for victory, began to appear on the walls of Paris. Ernst Van't Hoff and his Dutch orchestra performed a sneaky arrangement with lightly muted brass playing slightly altered three-dots-and-a-dash 'V for Victory' figures in several keys.

A grenade was tossed into a restaurant frequented by Germans, followed by a bloody reprisal.

The Jimmie Lunceford band cancelled a tour of France.

16
La Tristesse de Saint Louis

On the Côte d'Azur in the autumn of 1940, Charles Delaunay received a letter from a friend in Paris who told him that all of a sudden the city was jazz-crazy. On his way north, passing through Dijon, he saw posters announcing concerts by Fred Adison and Alix Combelle. Odd, jazz had rarely left the capital before the war. The hall was packed, the applause deafening.

He organized a concert in the Salle Gaveau on 19 December. All the big French names were on the bill, including Django Reinhardt and his new quintet with Hubert Rostaing. It sold out.

But Delaunay was impressed with more than numbers. Before the war, 'tout Paris' in tuxedos and gowns fell asleep to Duke Ellington in a sold-out Salle Pleyel. Now the audience was young, energetic, happy – the solidarity was palpable. He repeated the same programme a few nights later and it also sold out.

He had read Mein Kampf, he had no illusions about Hitler: 'I knew that sooner or later the Nazis would ban jazz, which they did after the United States entered the war.'

Delaunay emphasized in interviews and articles that jazz was now an international phenomenon, a mixture of European (French first), African, Latin and Anglo-Saxon influences. He told the musicians to go on playing the same songs, whatever they liked. Just change the names.

So 'St Louis Blues' became 'La Tristesse de Saint Louis', 'Honeysuckle Rose' 'La Rose de Chèvrefeuille', 'Sweet Sue' 'Ma Chère Susanne', and everybody went on swinging just like before. Well, almost . . .

17
Zazou Hey!

An aperitif named 'Swing' came on the market during the German occupation of France, not such a swinging time. 'Etes-Vous Swing?' and 'Mon Heure de Swing' were hit songs. The sartorial fad modelled after Cab Calloway's zoot suits was called 'Swing', the youngsters who wore it, 'Les Petits Swings', came to be known as 'Zazous', after Calloway's scat-singing syllables . . . zazouzazou – hey!

Zazou boys wore pegged pants with baggy knees, high rolled English collars covered by their hair, which was carefully combed into a two-wave pompadour over their foreheads, long checked jackets several sizes too large, dangling key chains, gloves, stick-pins in wide neckties with tiny knots; dark glasses and Django Reinhardt moustaches were the rage. The girls wore short skirts, baggy sweaters, pointed painted fingernails, hair curled to their shoulders, necklaces around their waists, bright red lipstick. Both sexes smoked Lucky Strike cigarettes, frequented 'Le New York Bar', and greeted each other: 'ça swing!'

They spent a lot of time in cafes, on the Champs Elysées or in the Latin Quarter. The Zazous on the Champs Elysées came from 'better' families. On Sundays they took portable gramophones to little exurban restaurants, played their swing records loud and danced. While dancing the one partner or another occasionally pointed fingers towards the sky and shouted 'ZAZOUZAZOU-ZAZOU. . .'

Swing became a password. To swing was really zazou. Hip. Chic. *Chouette*. Groovy. Singer Johnny Hess was crowned 'King of Swing', even more ersatz royalty than Benny Goodman, that other 'King of Swing'. Two white kings for black music. 'Les Petits Swings' related to swing, the music, like hippies later related to bebop. Image rather than substance. A cheap replacement. Ersatz.

Swing described a state of mind as well as music. Swing was one of the few things a youngster with any imagination and spirit could believe in. They certainly had little reason to believe in the Maréchal, their parents or the Germans. Many years later the hippies would say: 'You can't trust anyone over thirty.'

When the press insulted them ('what must the Germans think of our youth?'), they were amused. Becoming a Zazou was an amusing way to annoy the decidedly unamusing adult generation, the Germans particularly. Zazous were mostly from middle-class families, like hippies. One populist journal commented on the 'stupid Anglo-Saxon tendencies of this bourgeois youth already stupid by heredity'.

The Zazous were fond of kitsch, which involves unmasking pretentiousness and elevating mediocrity to an art form. Pétain's Vichy was classic kitsch. Hitler's moustache was kitsch. Chamberlain umbrellas and bowler hats were kitsch. Wearing a yellow star was kitsch if you were not Jewish.

The Zazous took nothing seriously. They opposed the regime by ignoring it, which was a political act whether they knew it or not. Wearing long jackets with wide collars and plenty of pleats is a political provocation during a highly publicized campaign for sartorial austerity.

From time to time the police would raid a Zazou cafe and take them to the prefecture. They would be questioned and have their papers and addresses checked. Some were sent to the countryside to help with the harvest, after a haircut of course. One newspaper wrote: 'We are of the opinion that when the rest of the continent is fighting and working, the Zazous' laziness is shameful. The young men without their hair or collars now are going to get healthy sweating in the July sun, the girls will soon have thicker ankles, freckles on their sweet noses and calluses on their dainty hands. And then the world will be back to its natural order.'

Intellectuals began to appreciate the Dadaistic virtues of the Zazous and, despite predictions that the Zazou subculture was disappearing, it eventually surfaced into the mainstream, like hippy culture. The show in Chez Eve on Place Pigalle was called *Zazou Zazou*. *Le Swing de l'Amour* was 'the review of the year' at Club l'Etincelle. And Le Moulin Rouge launched a heavily publicized spectacle, *Femmes et Rythmes – en deux actes hot et swing*. The film *Mademoiselle Swing* broke all records on the Champs Elysées.

Zazous were considered decadent by Germans and French alike. They were also bringing a lot of heat down on the music whose name 'Les Petits Swings' had co-opted. 'We tried to keep our distance from the Zazous,' recalls Charles Delaunay, who later would keep his distance from hippies too.

The Hot Club produced concerts, sponsored lectures, cut records and published their magazine throughout the occupation – though with shortages of paper, ink and printing facilities and a certain amount of political heat the magazine dropped its English title and appeared in shortened form on the back of concert programmes. In 1941, Delaunay wrote: 'The interpretation some give to swing is becoming dangerous for our music, their abuses risk leading to the banning of jazz itself. . .'

Hoping to avoid repression, he went on to criticize 'a turbulent, uneducated youth which, under the pretext of being swing, thinks itself permitted the worst excesses'.

Johnny Hess the King of Swing called a meeting of the Bowler Hat Club in a cafe on the Champs Elysées and fifty Zazous showed up with the English upper-class symbol on their heads. Like Jerry Rubin's Yippies burning money on the stock exchange, not a bad number. Maybe this was not such an ersatz king after all. *Ça swing,* your majesty.

Les Jeunesses Populaires Françaises, a French version of the Hitler Youth, sent out an appeal for volunteer barbers to shave the Zazous, although some were beginning to cut their hair on their own by then, to dress 'normally' and join a more direct and dangerous resistance.

Propaganda by definition aims at convincing anybody of anything, or everybody of everything. Delaunay had learned a few licks from the master Goebbels. For one thing, a moving target is hard to hit. Confuse the enemy, keep changing your address. He weaved and bobbed amid a flurry of punches in all directions: 'We are alarmed by the direction jazz has been taking,' he wrote in *Jazz Hot* in 1941:

Let us talk about the decadence which is unfortunately becoming increasingly apparent in the country of its birth. We see jazz degenerating in the United States. The Americans were the last to appreciate the importance and originality of this art form that was born on their own soil. Then they exploited its commercial side as only the Americans can do. They overlooked their major talents in favour of journeymen who could make more money playing music that bears only a superficial resemblance to jazz. Good and bad can have superficial similarity and the mediocre can be made to seem very attractive if helped by enough publicity.

Armstrong is already being forgotten in favour of those with more technique and superficial flash. They call genuine inspiration 'crude' because they have lost contact with real spiritual values. Jazz has finally entered our *moeurs*. It has become important to many of us and at first glance this ought to satisfy the majority of its defenders. But popular success is not enough. The new crowd listens like sports fans watch a boxer or a bicycle racer. They applaud the drummer's speed or the high note of a trumpet player. Knowledgeable fans view this tendency towards exhibitionism with consternation. To fight it, we are organizing a series of conferences to explain and analyse the art of jazz.

'Swing' is not scientific. A musician either has the gift or he doesn't. Swing is the only really new element jazz has brought to music, but it is a major revolution because swing can reach a complex, intense level of creativity . . .

Jazz combines innocence with sophistication. Born outside the conservatory, it broke many rules. This does not mean 'anything goes'. When a real artist mocks the rules it is because he is inventing another game, other rules, and these rules must be in accordance with nature, form, harmony and colour. The equilibrium can be strangled to death by too much analysis. Creativity cannot be taught; jazz has proved this once again. Pedagogy is sterile. Jazz is fresh and pure. The creator has only his instrument, his love and his unique personality for baggage. There are potentially as many variations of a style as there are individual human personalities. New Orleans style is the music made by people who come from that city and can be recognized just as easily as the southern accent of a person from the Midi. But let us reserve stylistic analysis for some other time. Right now we only want to proclaim the goal of the Hot Club de France

– the development of 'Jazz Français'.

In his book *Histoire Générale du Swing* published in Paris in 1942, André Coeuroy tried to prove that jazz was European rather than African, that it descended from French and Italian folk melodies and from Debussy: 'It has been assumed for a long time that jazz is specifically Negro music. My theory is the opposite. Jazz became Negro by chance. The principal elements are not only white, but European. Its history and its material both belong to us . . .'

Compromise in the name of survival has its limits. Delaunay reviewed Coeuroy's book in *Jazz Hot*: 'The author does not know his subject. It is just a superficial mass without unity. There are many contradictions and errors. Perhaps to try and remain in step with the current political state of affairs, the author adopted a thesis which he pushed to the absurd. He tries to prove that everything worthwhile in jazz is European, he portrays Negroes as clowns, he ridicules black music. This is really shocking. . .'

Delaunay's concert programmes either left the word 'jazz' out completely or qualified it as 'Jazz Français'. He told the Germans that jazz had French roots in the form of traditional New Orleans creole airs, and that, for example, 'Tiger Rag' was based on 'Praline', a nineteenth-century quadrille. The Germans wanted French collaboration and they went out of their way to respect French culture: 'There were a lot of Germans who liked jazz. They may have suspected what was going on, but they had more pressing worries. We used to have jam sessions in our cellar on rue Chaptal and one German officer often came to sit in on piano. He knew a lot of Fats Waller tunes. He couldn't do that in Germany.'

Yes he could, even in a concentration camp, as we know. He could also keep up with the latest news from abroad if he read the clandestine newsletter produced by Schulz-Koehn, Hans Bluthner, Otto Jung and their friends. Schulz-Koehn wrote:

Time does not stand still, even during war. There has been a lot of recent activity in the recording industry, particularly in foreign countries. New styles are being born, new talent is coming of age. Very little is heard about all this, and then much of it is false.

HOT CLUB DE FRANCE

FESTIVAL DE JAZZ FRANÇAIS

PROGRAMME
SALLE GAVEAU
PRIX : 5 FRANCS

Note: 'Jazz Français'

SALLE PLEYEL

LE HOT CLUB DE FRANCE

présentera

DIMANCHE

8

MARS

à 14 h. 30

ANDRE EKYAN

et son Swingtette

en attraction :

EDDIE BARCLAY

IMPROVISATIONS

avec :

ALEX RENARD ◆ CH. HARY

CH. WAGNER

PAUL COLLOT ◆ J. REINHARDT

M. SPEILEUX ◆ P. FOUAD

PRIX DES PLACES :

de **10** à **40** francs

....

Réductions aux Membres du H.C.F.

LOCATION :

SALLE PLEYEL, 252, Faubourg St-Honoré ;
HAMM, 133, Rue de Rennes ; PALAIS
DU DISQUE ET DE LA RADIO, Boule-
vard des Italiens ; DURAND, Place de
la Madeleine et au **HOT CLUB DE
FRANCE**, 14, Rue Chaptal

Concert programme from 1942. Note: the word 'jazz' does not appear. Eddie
Barclay, then a young pianist, is now president of Barclay Records

I am fortunate enough to be able to travel to the occupied countries of western Europe, and because of my professional standing I get many catalogues and letters from Sweden, Switzerland, Holland, Belgium and France. Sometimes messages even arrive from across the Channel or the Atlantic. I meet many specialists, musicians and jazz fans. So from time to time I will write travel letters. Many people have asked me to write about the jazz scene in these places, to pass information along to our friends.

And this we will do. But once we decided to go ahead with our project, we were faced with two problems. What to write about and who to send it to. We also asked ourselves whether it was proper to write anything at all about swing or hot music.

In the first place I want to make it clear that this question only applies inside the Fatherland. At the war front, outside the Reich, our soldiers can hear all the modern dance music they like, either live or over army radio. It is considered good for morale... If the general public at home is not permitted to hear this music, we can assume it is for a good reason and we accept it. But the distribution of our newsletter will be extremely limited and we will discuss only music and so it cannot be considered propaganda.

Schulz-Koehn continued:

Many young people, so-called 'Zazous', seek out American music just because it is forbidden, as a protest rather than for the music itself. We do not want to have anything to do with them. Real swing fans, on the other hand, are dedicated and honest. Even though most are young, they have a surprisingly positive attitude and a deep knowledge of classical music as well. I myself own about fifty recordings of classical music, particularly the two main forms that reached their highest level in Germany – the sonata with its drama and intricate structure, and the fugue with its incredible combination of music, fantasy and mathematics. Hot music has instrumental colour on one side and improvisational excitement on the other, it is also a highly creative art. Here we will not concern ourselves with banal hits, with silly lyrics, but only with instrumental improvisation. By the way, improvisation has interested serious composers for centuries.

Now the question of to whom these messages will be sent. They are limited in number, the circle is extremely narrow. This must be a club with functions similar to the Hot Club of France – promoting greater understanding of the music through lectures and conferences, listening to new records, organizing concerts. This music needs the support of radio and we hope one day, after the war, radio time will be given to us. Swing music is neither sensational nor erotic but a source of joy and it hurts me to realize how few people realize this.

There will be discographies of musical giants like Benny Carter, Artie Shaw, Fletcher Henderson and Duke Ellington. Photos, caricatures and drawings will provide a pleasant setting. We will discuss new bands and old ones, the latest record releases. There will be a bulletin board with announcements by people who would like to exchange records.

Similar information for classical music lovers is already plentiful. But swing music is new and I hope that our pages will fulfil a need and will be received with open arms and cherished.

In the 17 December 1984 issue of the *New Republic* ('Hipness at Noon'), Josef Skvorecky deals with a similar newsletter that had just been banned in Czechoslovakia. Suspected of being 'Czechs who liked syncopation more than their government', the Jazz Section of the Czech Musicians' Union was, however, legal. It had been created in 1971, three years after the 'Prague Spring', and was limited to 3,000 members. The leaders, who staged concerts and festivals and clinics and published a magazine, were enthusiastic unpaid volunteers. The members supported them enthusiastically. It was all a bit too enthusiastic.

Name the brand of totalitarian who said (about youngsters of whose manner of dress he disapproves): '...animals that bear only a superficial likeness to human beings'. Skvorecky says that exact phrase (by Czech Comrade Beran, about punks) was used by Streicher about Zazous in the pages of the newspaper *Der Sturmer*. Beran goes on: 'Command these crowds of half-wits, adorned with their cowbells and chains, to form columns and make them march in the direction of the foundries ...

The section's magazine became the haven for authors, artists and theorists of art interested in genres and trends that were, for all practical purposes, outlawed'. The magazine's series of art monographs, named 'Situaces' (situations) focused on what 'Dr Goebbels would call "entartete" '.

The section also published a paperback book series which included 'a fascinating study of how the Jews of the Terezin ghetto, facing death, managed to lead a far more cultural life than the Wagner-adoring Nazis could ever boast of'. The series included several studies of Western rock, an essay (including a discography) about Gary Burton, photographs of the graffiti on Prague's John Lennon wall, and other works on the frontier of dissidence.

Although Schulz-Koehn's newsletter avoided capital 'P' politics and was limited to only fifty or so 'friends', the principle is the same. A loophole. Skvorecky estimates that the magazine had about 100,000 readers before the banning of the section's festival, 'Prague Jazz Days', along with the magazine and the section itself.

Fascist Germany cannot be separated from Socialist Czechoslovakia and fascist Sad Afrika; Zazous from hippies or punks. People of good will always refer back when something bad happens and say, 'It's just like Nazi Germany.' The Third Reich has become a common reference for evil.

Jean-Marie Le Pen's far-right National Front has been compared with the early Nazi party and French working-class anti-Arab and -black racism is on the rise. Political analysts agree that, like the Nazis, the National Front vote is coming largely from disgruntled, often unemployed, Communists. While Socialist policemen frequently verify papers and search blacks and Arabs in the metro.

Claude Verses avoids certain heavily controlled stops, when he dares take the metro at all. For-hire taxis pass him by. He was not at all surprised to be 'asked' to leave that restaurant; it's happened before – although he did not expect to be languishing in jail.

His German woman threw him out. Several nights later, he came back with a spare key, stole her undeclared cash savings and, so she told the police, raped her. There being no habeas corpus in this country, he has been in La Santé prison for several months now. His woman moved back to Germany and has neither returned to testify nor withdrawn charges. When I went to the US embassy to see what I could do for him, the officer I talked to turned out to be one of Claude's old Girl clients. 'It's out of my jurisdiction,' he said.

The fact that his woman was German is neither invented by me nor insignificant to Verses, who wrote from jail: 'What is it you once told me about "re-enacting symbolic deeds of sinister significance"? Who wrote it? Please send the exact quote. I am "letting time serve me serving time" as they used to say in Attica ... trying to write something, it's hard to describe, but basically I think I can establish a connection between – now don't laugh – Klaus Barbie and the Barbie doll.'

Once more we come to the definition of the subject. Sticking to 'the subject' is bad form. Only the widest defensible definition is adequate. Everything is interlinked, including the life that surrounds the writing of these words. The bio of the author on the jacket is part of the book.

'Dr Toro-Merde is currently professor of Genital Torture at the University of Higher Lying, he has been awarded the Julius Streicher Memorial Fellowship by the Wilddeath Society and is working on a book entitled *Copping Out: a Viable Alternative.*'

That may seem a bit extreme but it seems to me that extreme is the only way to be. Django was extreme; George Scott was extreme. It is a way to survive during extreme times.

I once read a critique of an article about a documentary film of a director shooting the stageplay *Macbeth*, during which the director turned his camera around and shot the documentary film-maker shooting him. Finally there was a long letter from a reader in a later issue of the same magazine criticizing the critique of the article about the documentary about the feature film of the play.

Back to the main matter at hand. ('At last!' you might be excused for exclaiming.) A schoolteacher named Henri Vémane wrote a book titled *Swing et Moeurs*, published in Lille, France, during the summer of 1943, in which he analysed jazz and swing with a bizarre combination of Catholicism, Marxism, Socialism and ecological concern. More passionate than logical, it is an astonishing book to have been published under a fascist regime. Extracts follow:

This nervous, grotesque, eccentric music is original, it must be admitted, but so what? Is originality automatically desirable? Shouldn't we be more concerned with pruning our roots than growing disorderly branches? What are its antecedents and implications? I seem to be raising questions rather than providing answers. Let us go back to the beginning and pursue our research with scientific impartiality.

The revolutions of the eighteenth century overthrew political institutions. In the nineteenth the industrial revolution irrevocably changed the nature of work. The steam engine multiplied the strength of man a hundred times. The first locomotives date from the reign of Louis-Philippe. These ugly monsters gradually replaced the horse and carriage and people were free to travel longer distances more frequently.

But industry was the first to profit as mechanical power replaced muscle power. Giant steel melting furnaces were built next to the coal mines. Volume was the key to industrial viability and ever larger factories devastated our countryside. They replaced the small workshops passed down through generations of families belonging to the same guild. Working men began to bring their families to the teeming cities and took jobs in factories which spewed carbonic fumes and filth.

The machine inaugurated a reign of terror of its own. The working man was trapped like a fish in the tentacles of an octopus. The success of a factory depended on the amount of working capital it could muster. Even the largest private fortunes were soon insufficient. Rich families fusing their assets soon gave birth to the system known as capitalism.

The psyche of the working man was swallowed without pity in this period of tumultuous change. Many employers were unscrupulous in the name of profit and ambition. It was a new form of slavery in the name of progress. Exploited, isolated, powerless, the working man was gradually transformed into something called 'the proletariat'.

Interesting as this socio-political exposition may be, the reader is probably asking, 'But what does it have to do with swing?' Patience, I beg you.

The machine gradually replaced the working man, who was reduced to a mere button-pusher. He spent ten hours a day in the middle of a noisy, filthy fracas. His senses were constantly assaulted. Though he continued to control the work-process in the sense that without him there could be no work, the machine was nevertheless the boss and the working man became a victim. His nervous system was torn asunder by the vibrations of the factory. The exigencies of the production line left him no time to relax. Soon he became a kind of machine himself. The principal cadence of his life became mechanical. This is the cadence now called 'Swing'.

Crushed and worn out by his work, oppressed by unscrupulous bosses, menaced by unemployment and hunger, the worker tried to find temporary escape from his misery. Not finding anything in himself or his home to ease the pain, he looked for it in bars. He played games with his buddies. He laughed. He drank. He became a wino. Alcohol, like the factory, causes nervous disorder. He escalated to whisky. The worker needed ever-increasing doses of excitement. He discovered jazz. I do not have scientific justification to draw a parallel between alcohol and swing, but Americans are known to be big whisky-drinkers and jazz is their music. It is something to think about.

Then came war. Explosions, detonations, debris, fatigue, fear and hysteria. Civilians went to sleep at night not sure they would wake up in the morning. Imagine the state of a fighter pilot's nervous system. We are talking about a major biological imbalance which led to the schizophrenic rhythms of swing, the perfect reflection of our imperfect times.

The working class now wanted to be freed from the chains of what I call 'Machinism', even though they had welcomed the machine fifty years earlier as a liberator which was going to reduce the work week, the work load, and lead them to luxury everywhere. But their horizon has been reduced to little corners of the sky still visible through the smokestacks and scrap piles.

Atheistic politicians exploit the situation. Do not look to the 'opium of the people' for salvation. Enough resignation, enough working as a duty or for charity. Enough turning the other cheek. The proletariat has a right to happiness. Now. But how to get it? Only one way – force. 'Death to the capitalists.' The working man will inherit the leather easy chairs.

This is the worldly paradise for the working man according to Karl Marx, Engels and their school. Their new order is based on material values. They deny God and the soul as contrary to their hypothesis. They look for salvation to the very machine that brought us to this hell in the first place. This reasoning is a threat to reason itself. But people who are suffocating will do anything in order to breathe. So for generations we have lived in the shadow of shaky material happiness.

A *chanson* that was popular a few years ago went like this: 'Let's amuse ourselves, go crazy, Life is so short...' Isn't that ideal? Take what you can get here and now. Worry about later later. Sensations first, the spirit can wait. And so we come back to jazz, a voluptuous music which springs from the senses, the 'expression of the moment' we are told. *Voilà*. From 'Machinism' to swing.

At war, we risk death daily. 'We may well lose our lives before having lived them. Let us profit from the moment, enjoy our youth, satisfy our passion. Live today, forget about tomorrow.' That is how swing was born.

Modern young men and women feel that they have the right to be freer than their parents. They feel that they relate to each other with 'fresh simplicity'. Fine, let's not discuss it. It's one possible version. 'We are only doing honestly in the open what our parents did with shame in the closet,' they say. In the twentieth century love is born, grows up and dies in a day. They kiss in the tram, in the movies, at the theatre. They have no shame. They say it is not up to us to judge them.

This libertinism runs parallel to the alienation of youth from parents. Today's 'kids' are impossible. They take three months' vacation for granted; you don't dare criticize them. I hear that sort of thing all the time from parents. I'm a teacher, I'm well-placed to hear it. The nervous instability of our children is difficult to deal with. They encounter and toy with impurity at an early age. In working-class schools in particular, it is not unusual to find totally perverted eight-year-olds.

Whose fault is it? The cinema has a lot to answer for. The dizzy cadence of images damages both the retina and the nervous system. So many films are immoral. Debauchery is more frequent than virtue. You hear questions like, 'Why did the lady dance with that Monsieur? Why didn't that little baby have a father?' How about the following true dialogue between Gérard, nine, and his aunt?

'You know something, auntie?'

'What, my darling?'

'I'm Swing and you're Zazou.'

'What does that mean, darling?'

'I don't know, but that's the way it is.'

We have to close our ranks and fight our common enemy, swing. Rhythm rhythm more rhythm, from fast to faster, life moves at a crazy speed. After ten centuries of culture, we end with the Negro jungle tom-tom. Nervous, excited, shouting, crying. Swing, an explosion of insanity.

Our body is composed of billions of microscopic cells, each of which is in turn composed of atoms. Each cell is in fact a complex factory. The nervous system provides the electricity to run it. This grid of factories guards our health. Now you can understand the seriousness of too much tension on the cells. One grain of sand can cause a short circuit. Swing is a grain of sand in the gears.

Swing plunges the subject into constant excitement. It causes nightmares. You get addicted to it. It's like drugs. You say, 'I'll just listen once to see what it's like.' You need more and more. The final result is a significant lowering of the intelligence. You cannot juggle with the body's equilibrium like ping-pong balls. Swing represents the victory of passion over reason.

When you are 'swing' you have no morals. I do not want to exaggerate, but think about it. Did you know that 100,000 Frenchmen die each year from syphilis? Did you know that in the same period of time, 100,000 little Frenchmen never see the light of day because of abortions? Now we cannot blame swing for every monstrosity, but we can deduce that the young men and women who admire or practise this Negroid eccentricity help establish a cause and effect between Zazouism and immorality.

Since 1940 France has been defeated and impotent. This is one of the most tragic periods of its history. One hundred thousand of its sons lost their lives on the battlefield. And yet today there is a line in front of every cinema. Theatres are full. The elderly are dying of hunger trying to live on 100 francs a month, ghostly silhouettes are picking food from garbage cans, and yet banknotes are flying out of billfolds in the Zazou Bar.

Because of its materialist origin, swing is often an antagonist of religion. 'Nobody is able to serve two masters.' Having a weak spot for Zazouism inevitably leads to a loss of contact with God.

Nervous eccentricity, as we have seen, devours the subject by a general pitiless fever. When you spend Saturday night in an illegal dancehall, there is no energy left for Sunday-morning mass. Passion destroys charity.

Result: criminality, debauchery, HATE. Nervousness, eccentricity and pleasure are the three principal characteristics of swing – the trilogy of today's youth.

I am not a fanatic, prejudiced or narrow-minded. I am not a moralist. I am not God, I cannot see into the future. But wasn't it the worship of physical pleasure that caused the fall of the Roman empire? Every civilization since the beginning of history has fallen. Ruins everywhere. Why should European civilization be an exception? I will not finish by accusing swing of being at the root of all our faults. But I will denounce the danger it poses. With the risk of being called a pessimist, I do suggest that swing is one manifestation of the decline of our civilization.

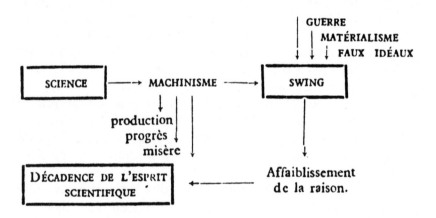

18
The Bête Noire

How did Django relate to all of that polemic? Probably not at all. Reading about swing would not have interested him. His mind was preoccupied with his fingers. In any case, I could not find a trace of a statement on the state of the music or his aesthetic philosophy, unless you consider, 'Jazz attracted me because it has a perfection of form and instrumental precision worthy of the great masters, and which you do not find in other kinds of popular music' philosophical.

He became my *bête noire*. I've been pecking away, you may have noticed, cautiously, a little at a time. Sneaking up on him. It's scary. He always sneaks up on me. I know, he's dead; that's the scariest part.

Writing biographical material about Django Reinhardt reminds me of the time I interviewed Bob Dylan. It's heavy, better get it right. The World Series. Keep your eye on the ball. Plenty of sliders. Just try and get on base. The pitcher is not going to give you a fat one down the middle. Django seems to have been even less talkative than Dylan, if that's possible. I clipped, read more articles and books, interviewed people a second time, interviewed new people. I was coming up with information like: 'He was really a fantastic guy', or, 'I don't remember', and 'You know, he was not like other people'.

I began to realize the absurdity of it. He was a Gypsy. They are not known for talking straight with *Gajo* reporters. I remember something Rafael told me, parenthetically, just a pause for breath really: 'Never trust anything a Gypsy tells you.' Anyway, there was no need for word talk, old Maccaferri-mouth.

It is said that one disappears 'like a Gypsy into the night'. You wake up and your hero is gone, rode off into the sunset, as Lenny Bruce used to say in his Lone Ranger routine, 'without waiting for a "thank you masked man"'. It took me a while, perhaps too long a while, to realize that the mask alone was a key clue; that my inability to 'find' him was not any fault of mine, but an insight into *him*.

He went through millions of francs during the war, ending up with nothing. He could be rich one day, broke the next. Broke, not even a bank account. He never grew up. 'How old was Django?' asks Yves Salgues in *Jazz* magazine:

> The age of a virgin forest. There is no figure to fit his age. You can rather describe his time as 'the age of Django'. If you were to tell him to look out or he will finish life as a bum, he would answer: 'I started as a Gypsy and I'll finish as a Gypsy.' To change him, you might as well try and make an Eskimo live in Sicily. Django Reinhardt was not a 'citizen', he was a 'creature'.

The 'creature' once told a friend one of his fantasies: 'If I was rich I'd live in New York. I'd have a bungalow - not a skyscraper, a beautiful bungalow. I'd have the best cognac and a beautiful billiard table. I would not do anything, just play a little music from time to time to become even richer. I'd live like anybody else who owned a gold mine or an oil well - like Ford, Rockefeller, Rubirosa. I'd go to a concert by the Boston Symphony in the afternoon. The melodies of the classical composers are so beautiful - Bach, my brother Bach, Beethoven, Stravinsky. I would dine in a very expensive restaurant on the island of Manhattan. A penthouse restaurant high in the sky. It would be like owning the city. A calm restaurant. Eating good food, it is better not to be hurried. That is very bad for the stomach. That's why there would be sweet music in the restaurant. Glenn Miller is good for the digestion. After coffee and a digestif, I'd leave for Harlem because dancing is very good for the digestion too. That's why I'd like to go to Harlem after dinner to dance to the good swing music of my black brothers.'

He often lost playing billiards or poker, lost enormous sums of money betting on himself, because although he was a champion he challenged other champions to prove he was the very best, which he was not. Pockets bulging with cash flattened before many dawns.

He loved children. One day he was visiting a friend, playing with his young grandson. The concierge came up and knocked on the door saying there was a telephone call for Mr Reinhardt on her phone (the only phone in the building at the time). It was his agent, she said, and it sounded urgent. Django said he was busy right now and to tell the agent he would call back. The friend suggested that he should perhaps take the call, it might mean an engagement, and he could play with his grandson later. Django said: 'Children should never be kept waiting.'

He moved from rue des Acacias to a house in Villa Frochot, near the corner of rue Victor Massé, next door to the house of Pierre Renoir, the painter's son, an actor who had a wife and two children. Django played darts with the Renoir children in their back yard, or strummed a guitar and watched the children play.

He liked the neighbourhood because it was close to the Pigalle metro stop, the deepest and thus presumably safest in Paris. Delaunay calls him a '*peureux*', scaredy-cat. With the first hint of trouble, the first wail of the air-raid warning, he'd dash down there as fast as possible, women and children last.

Yet there was no reproach, not even a hint of an accusation of cowardice from Delaunay. It was just a quirk, like showing up late or not showing up at all. People seemed ready to accept just about any eccentricity from this man. When Django had his photo taken with a Luftwaffe officer, or played with or for Germans, there was never a question of collaboration. He was exempt from the rules somehow. When he had Joseph carry his guitar, nobody accused him of being spoiled, playing the star. Although he gambled, drank and womanized, I never once heard him called decadent.

'Naïve, childlike', is how the Belgian saxophonist and bandleader Fud Candrix described him: 'He loved shiny things. When he was in Brussels during the war, he walked around town wearing a cowboy hat, a red scarf with white polka dots, white leather shoes and a shiny bright blue suit. Obviously everybody stared at him, but he did not do these things to attract attention. He was just like a child wearing a costume. It was a game to him. Life was a game to him.'

And guitarist René Thomas said: 'Django was a champion of the guitar, he was a billiard champion. He was a champion at anything he did.'

A relatively obscure cult hero before the war, he became a megastar overnight. People whistled 'Nuages' on the street and his name was on the walls of Paris. 'He was as well-known as Maurice Chevalier,' says Delaunay. 'When he came to a town for a concert, people knew that something happy was going to happen for a change.'

There were no more American films, no touring American stars of stage, screen and radio, no more American jazzmen. Of course there was Tino Rossi, Piaf, Chevalier and the others, but the Germans *liked* them. They liked them a bit too much. It was at least embarrassing if not collaboration. But they hated swing; swing was fun, and nobody in the world swung better than 'Made in France' Django Reinhardt. So swing it would be.

Demand for swing music was so great that sidemen quickly became leaders, Saturday-night amateurs full-time sidemen. The Americans had gone home, competition was light, just about any European jazzman who could blow a chorus of the blues had all the work he could handle.

But listening to Django's wartime records, you are struck with a man playing with boys. Names like André Ekyan, Philippe Brun, Alix Combelle and Hubert Rostaing are mentioned in the same breath as Django but they are like flat-footed minor-league baseball players kicked up into the big leagues through the ravages of the draft. There was Django and then everybody else.

Stephane Grappelli, who could keep up with Django but who spent the war in London, spoke of this in one of our interviews: 'He was wasting his talent, I saw him throwing it out. I would often try to argue him out of wasting his time playing cards or some such nonsense. I'd say, "Come on, man, let's go somewhere and compose a song. A good one, something that will last for a while." Hopeless. But you know, he didn't drink very much. It wasn't that. Music was enough for us; we'd get drunk with it. We played together, just the two of us, very often because the rest of the musicians were incapable of following us. Django really suffered from that. We had a lot of trouble finding adequate bassists, for example. He couldn't stand wrong notes. They would traumatize him. He considered wrong notes a personal insult.'

During the cold April of 1942, Django went to Belgium for a

concert at the Palais des Beaux Arts sponsored by the Hot Club de Belgique which had just changed its name to Club Rythmique de Belgique after the authorities banned the English language.

The occasion was a world premiere, the Fud Candrix orchestra playing an arrangement of Django's composition, 'Bolero'. Django bought a white suit and a conductor's baton, a long one, maybe forty centimetres long. He wanted to conduct but he could not read music and had no idea how to wave a baton.

'Hey Fud,' Django said during the rehearsal. 'How do you work this thing? How does "one, two, three, four" go? From high to low or low to high, from right to left or left to right?'

Candrix showed him . . . down left right up. Django practised, Candrix coached him again during intermission but he mounted the podium shaking and unsure. Directly in front, down in the saxophone section, Candrix prompted him but Django limited himself to tiny timid strokes in front of his body so the audience could not see any mistakes. Of course the musicians couldn't see anything either.

Django was the cosmic improviser, all instinct; he could do what very few others could do: make up his own rules. He made music conform to his instinct. There was just no way he could make a mistake. He didn't know it was a mistake to begin with. He could stretch 'one two three four', compress it, turn it around and upside down and compared to all that, beating it with a stick is meaningless. But tuxedos and batons represent class, and he had respect for class. It infuriated him that he could not play this particular game.

Candrix repeated the same programme the following night. But when intermission was announced, Django had not yet arrived. They called the Grand Hotel. He was not in his room. The intermission was prolonged. Somebody thought to look for him in the hotel restaurant, where he was found eating. He said he thought the concert was tomorrow night. Since taxis were out of the question in those days, they ran to the hall and Django walked out on stage forty-five minutes late with his guitar and that shit-eating grin of his, flashy white teeth a dramatic contrast with his trademark pencil-line black moustache. The audience applauded and with a guitar he was as much at ease on stage as playing poker. Playing guitar, like life, was a piece of cake.

While in Brussels, he recorded with the Stan Branders and Fud

Candrix bands in the studios of Radio Schaerbeek. There was no heating fuel in Belgium and it was cold in the studio. The pianist Yvon de Bie rehearsed with gloves on.

De Bie and Django had two duets. De Bie was not very proud of how he played. This was the date on which Django played violin. De Bie got lost trying to improvise without a rhythm section. He had already jammed with Django. He had not been very proud of what he played that time either. Frankly, playing with Django scared him. There was Django and then everybody else.

Later the same year, the Candrix orchestra gave four concerts in Paris at Salle Pleyel. Attendance was so good; two more were added. Candrix featured a small group from his band – accordion, violin, drums and bass. After 'Lady Be Good', Django, who was in the front row, rose arms in the air crying out, *'Bravo, Fud, c'est formidable!'* Applauding was not enough when Django Reinhardt liked something.

He invited the Candrix band to the Hot Club cave on rue Chaptal. They arrived just before 10.30 curfew time and listened to the French musicians. Django invited them to sit in.

'We'll play if you play,' Candrix said.

'No, you guys are too strong for me,' Django said, without a trace of irony.

Candrix insisted, but no dice.

There was a shortage of cigarettes in France; Django was a heavy smoker and Candrix had a pack of Amadis, a Belgian brand. Alix Combelle said: 'I'll bet he'll play for one pack of those.'

'Can I bribe you?' Candrix asked, pulling a pack of Amadis from his pocket. Django's eyes rolled around in their sockets, a wide smile spread on his face and they played until the curfew lifted at dawn.

A few days later in a recording studio, Candrix wanted Django to play on his arrangement of something he named 'ABC', the theatre where his band had just appeared, but it was a written arrangement and he knew Django could not read music.

Django said, 'That's OK, play it, I'll pick it up.'

Candrix thought putting it in an easier key might help. 'Would you rather play in B flat or F?' he asked.

'One of each,' Django answered. 'Let's *do* it.'

Candrix invited Django for a night of poker. They bought two bottles of fine Martel brandy at 500 francs each on the black market and played cards. As the brandy went down, they began to fool around singing the current American hit 'Idaho'. The Candrix band was playing it for Germans, having changed the title to 'Ida Oo Oo'. Drunk, wasting good hands losing money, Django began to amuse himself with the lyrics to 'Idaho' he had made up for a woman with a wide-brimmed hat who had blocked his view of a movie a few nights ago. Women's wide-brimmed hats were the rage. He couldn't see a thing, so he sang to her: *'Vous avez un beau chapeau, Madame, quel beau chapeau que vous avez.'*

A week or so after the poker game, the entire Candrix band stood up on the stage of the Grand Cafe Corso, on Boulevard Adolphe Sax, Brussels, turned to a woman wearing such a hat and sang: 'You have a beautiful hat, Madame, oh what a beautiful hat you have' to the tune of 'Ida Oo Oo.' Everybody laughed, including madame. It turned out to be the biggest hit of Candrix's career.

Gypsies in concentration camps tried to save themselves by claiming to be Django Reinhardt. A customer walked into Le Doyen to confront the 'phony' Django working there. He had known the real one in a camp. But listening for five minutes convinced him of his error; no two people could play the guitar like that.

Charles Delaunay tells a story about a Gypsy wedding to which Django invited the drummer Pierre Fouad, Hubert Rostaing and the other musicians with whom he was working in Chez Jane Stick. The wedding was just beginning to swing when it was time to go to work. Django said the rest of them could do fine without him that night. The party was just getting started. Afterwards he was so embarrassed he never did go back and the band finished the two-week engagement without him.

He was the star and there is no doubt that he felt it earned him a certain exemption. As his price went up, he felt no obligation to share the increase with sidemen. It was not so much being cheap as, well, princely. There was no logic in his money management. He'd ask for absolutely absurd figures and refuse to budge. Then the next night he would play for hours for free. Or he'd give Fouad 100 francs too much and be 100 short with Rostaing. But then nobody ever accused Django Reinhardt of being logical.

Fouad asked him how much he would be making for a record

date coming up. 'Three-fifty,' Django answered. Delaunay had just told Fouad that the going price was 400, and he complained. 'That's the way it goes,' Django shrugged, adding, 'How about a game of billiards after the date?'

'What handicap?' Fouad asked, cautiously.

'Oh fifteen or twenty points, or so.'

Fouad knew he wasn't worth more than fourteen at most. Django was always getting his figures wrong. He was just showing off. Fouad won close to 100,000 francs that night. Typical Django; chisel fifty here, lose 100,000 there.

Delaunay had been talking to me in the study of his luxurious house in Chantilly, a town known for horses and thick cream, though luxurious is not really the word. The house and its furnishings are too discreet for that. Luxury implies costly. 'Burnished' might be better: well worn, polished, a shine that takes years and effort to glow. Something so classic that age increases value. A burnished item might well have been inexpensive to begin with. And mere money cannot buy such taste. You either have a tasteful decorator or you are an artist, most likely a visual artist of some kind; art was in your blood before you got your money. Delaunay made his own money, but he paints and both his parents were famous artists who sold their art and so he lives within a tasteful combination of art and money that money alone can't buy.

I sat in his study reading wartime issues of *Jazz Hot* into a tape-recorder. He would not let them out of the house to be photocopied. It meant hours of reading. He sat next to me correcting my French as I read, from time to time placing items in context.

I had been in this house once before, for the first of our three interviews. Then he had taken me into his son's studio adjoining the house. His son paints in an abstract style. The paintings stored and being worked on in the studio are anguished, full of violent colours and contorted shapes and they reveal a spirit which is not at peace with itself. They reminded me of John Coltrane during his 'sheets of sound' period. The colours jump out, climb up the walls and out of the window. Delaunay shook his head and said he did not understand such an aesthetic. He also said he did not understand the music his son listened to, though he was by now resigned to it, or rather to escaping from it, for the rest of his life.

On my way out after reading the wartime *Jazz Hots*, we passed from the study through the living-room towards the door. Delaunay's son, a bright and friendly young blond man, was sitting in the living-room listening to *In a Silent Way* by Miles Davis – streamlined, modern jazz with a touch of rock – while watching a hardcore porn video with no sound. Embarrassed, he jumped up to switch the video off.

'No no,' Delaunay laughed. 'You can leave that. Turn the *music* off.'

19
My Blue Heaven

Overlooking the bright green and blue Mediterranean, the sun more white than red, leaning my bag of bones on ancient stones, I feel behind me the draft from a black tunnel. I had thought I'd never reach the end of it. Wobbly and squinting, I appear to have emerged on the side of the living. Perhaps the tunnel had been a simple 'mid-life crisis', though such a profoundly painful crawl is inadequately described by that trite phrase which somehow sneaked in here from *Time* magazine. A yellow sticker on my wall reads: 'The light at the end of the tunnel comes from the end you went in at.'

Svend Asmussen is looking at the deserted terrace of a cafe in this off-season hilltop Provençal town. Several months yearly in his clement, harmonious, remote, and, after decades of development, soulless paradise has cost him world-class standing. By doing the expected thing for someone his age, investing in sun-belt real estate, synchronizing his life with tax lawyer's tropic logic, he finds himself out of a game he is not nearly ready to stop playing. The star of occupied Danish jazz, fiddler Asmussen, who looks nowhere near sixty-nine, is still a star up there but not down here. He asked me for the name of a booking agent. Me. I could not help him. I lost my diary on the Bowery.

We are both under house arrest. Prisoners of arresting houses. Neither of us is in a position to pick up and take off. Let's go to Rome. Tonight. Remember?

But perhaps I only imagine his unhappiness. That's not even the worst of it. I think I imagine my own. Misery does not love company, it creates it.

No, no more of that. Your victory is no longer my loss, your loss is no longer my solace.

The children still ride their square-wheeled tricycles above our bedroom, and the noise of the elevator is still angry but France and I have begun to make love in it nevertheless. Though the roof still leaks, friends come for dinner, or, unannounced, for a nightcap by the fire in our hearth. The fire has attracted new friends. They help themselves to beer. The kilos have begun to reappear.

It's the old half-full/half-empty controversy resolved by the positive measure. She has grappled her way to the top of her ministry's hierarchy, climbed the sheer cliffs out of the snake pit on her own. Not even a piton. She has daily contact with the minister, who ministers to her sunny spirit like the asset it is and which we should never have depreciated. Over fifty and pushing forty, not such a bad daily double after all. The war is over.

Sighing with resignation and groaning with fear are two endless vamps, in flat keys yet. A vamp is one chord suspended indefinitely. The last chord. That seemed to be it for a while. That great big decrescendo in the sky. But I hear ascending changes. A consonant resolution.

Of course it's easy to talk about a happy ending so near to the last chapter. It was touch and go there for a while. Subjects were dying and declining all around me. Five more years and this process could not have taken place. Witnesses kept disappearing, twelve kilos of the prosecutor were even kidnapped. I hate to keep mentioning 'an article I read in today's *Herald Tribune*', and this particular coincidence may seem a bit convenient but the paper came late and I read it this evening before smoothing out this final draft...an obituary for Leopold Tyrmand, the Polish writer who sat next to the German soldier who told him that jazz made him think of free people. Under the wire. A hairsbreadth. A close shave. But we have come out of the tunnel and the snake pit and endless vamp.

Buddy Mary sent a peace treaty in an envelope: '...You're going to die one of these days. And Robbie is going to miss you. Do you want to leave the kid the image of a gaunt Dad who whines half the time and is bitterly depressed picking his pimples the other half? Don't you want to leave him something that gives him strength?

"The only thing that's keeping me alive is Robbie." You said that to me. But I don't believe it. If you really wanted to be here for and with Robbie you wouldn't have let your body get to the really dreadful state you've let it get to. You get much skinnier and keep whining, Bro, and I ain't gonna look at you no mo'.'

Robbie has been whining about the teacher in charge of his school canteen who always nags the kids to finish their plates by saying: 'Think of the starving children in Africa.' He tapped his temple with a forefinger three times, *'toc, toc, toc'*, like his comic-strip hero Obelix when he considers somebody nuts: 'I can't help it if I hate spinach.'

'Stop whining,' I said. 'Eat your spinach. Spinach is good for you.'

'If it's so good, you eat it.' He pushed the plate towards me.

I gulped it down: 'Think of all the starving jazz musicians in New York.'

France tried to frown but she's losing the habit: 'You're taking food out of the mouth of your growing child.'

'I'm a gaunt adult.'

She laughed. 'No, you're not. I have two children. One growing, one shrinking.' We all laughed. We laughed very hard for a long time.

'Piece of cake,' I said.

In Hamburg in 1939, Svend Asmussen was working in a snobby Anglophile restaurant specializing in scones. Sometimes a customer would send over a bottle of champagne with a request. 'Flat Foot Floogie mit ein Floy Floy' was popular that season.

When he went to Paris to spend the money he had earned in Hamburg, Asmussen saw the Eiffel Tower, all the museums, Versailles; and every night he would jam until dawn. He always carried his fiddle, and he was always invited to play it. Everywhere, it was the same, wherever he has been. In all the countries, musicians who improvise swing music together, they communicate. Straight people do not understand. They say, 'He's a terrible man. He beats up his wife, he gambles, he takes drugs,' but if he could swing it was always OK. Deep down, it was beautiful. That was the only important thing. Then another man, a dependable man, a good father, accepted by society, an honest man, but, well, somehow you just don't like him because he doesn't know how to swing.

A Norwegian singer, a big fat one, we won't mention his name, was like all the other musicians, defying the Nazis, he sang swinging songs in English. Musicians paid no attention to Nazi orders in Copenhagen. There had never been any doubt in Asmussen's mind: the Germans would lose the war. How could he take somebody who looked as corny as Hitler with that silly little moustache seriously? But this fat singer got it into his head that the Germans were winning and he went back to Norway and joined the party. After the war, Asmussen was taking a walk with his wife in a big park outside Oslo, they were alone in this huge landscape when they saw the singer – he was as fat as Fats Waller so you couldn't miss him – coming towards them. Asmussen said to his wife, 'that son of a bitch', and they walked right by each other without saying a word. It was a strange feeling because this singer knew how to swing.

It was a dilemma when German soldiers came into a place where Asmussen was playing and requested 'Honeysuckle Rose'. Then he'd think: what the hell, they can't help it if they've been drafted, they don't want to wear those uniforms. He did not want to be ice-cold with them like the other Germans. 'We're musicians,' they'd say. 'We buy your records.'

In 1941, Albert Bossen, a well-known German accordion player who could play pretty hot if he felt like it, was touring with a good guitarist named Frank Korseck in a German army band. Korseck had a beautiful big new Gibson guitar. It was just about impossible to find them in occupied Europe. Two weeks after their concert in Copenhagen, Korseck was sent to the Eastern front and was shot right away. No more Frank Korseck. The first thing that went through Asmussen's mind when he heard about it was, 'Whatever happened to that Gibson?'

By 1942 Asmussen's quintet was in demand. Their records, mostly American standards, were being sold all over Europe. They were played on the radio, even in neutral Sweden. When the band was offered a month at the top of the bill in the China Theatre in Stockholm, they were surprised to be granted a travel permit. But the Germans were still trying to be nice to the Danes. So the band took a boat from the blackouts, the curfew, the Jews disappearing in the night and it was like arriving on another planet – the lights were all on, you could buy anything you liked. Their combination of swing music and comedy routines broke all records in the China

Theatre. Asmussen's drummer at the time was really fine. His name was Frederick. He only had one name.

The following year Asmussen opened a jazz club. He named it 'My Blue Heaven', in English. Some of the customers were Danish Nazis, dangerous people, Quislings, they wore black uniforms, they'd give away their own grandmothers. When they requested a Viennese waltz and Asmussen said, 'Sorry, we don't play them, we play our own music', they complained to the authorities: 'You can tell by the name of this place what kind of music they play here', and the German patrols came: '*Vas iss Doss?* You play American jazz music?' Asmussen always managed to smoothe it out somehow.

Danish 'Swing Crazies' wore the same costume and hair-dos as the Zazous, they jitterbugged and were described by one journalist as 'an example of the depraved upper class and the result of too much permissiveness on the part of parents and teachers'. Swing Crazies would come into My Blue Heaven to dance from time to time and then Asmussen would have to smoothe that out too. His group was very popular with his upper-class clientele; the 'Swing Crazies' were not. When a new law said that you had to exchange ration cards for drinks, butter and meat, which was all ersatz anyway, it wasn't so good for the restaurant business.

Many recordings of thirties' Danish jazz were melted down during the war to be recycled and so musical evidence is meagre, though some critiques remain: 'It may be true that jazz is a distinguished art form but if so I haven't heard any jazz yet.'

Jazz Versus European Musical Culture, by Olaf Sobys (1935): 'Jazz was not born in nor has it ever been integrated into European culture. It was introduced from the violent need of a primitive race for rhythmic ecstasy and cannot grow organically here. It represents mankind's lowest bestial instincts. Jungle jazz rhythm is an expression of the primitive Negro's erotic ecstasy.' Ellington and Armstrong are 'monsters'; literally, ugly beasts, not a synonym for 'giants' as in contemporary argot. Jazz is 'a running sore on European culture': Sobys recommends amputation. 'The fact that the white race tolerates this sort of thing indicates our culture's decline. Denmark should follow Germany. When Hitler banned jazz, it was a great idealistic act.'

Cooler heads reflected that perhaps jazz has such a violent effect on people because it leads them to discover something primitive in their nature they are ashamed to admit to themselves. Jazz was central to the fascist/anti-fascist debate both before and during the occupation. Poul Henningsen's documentary film *Denmark* included a jazz soundtrack that was heavily criticized for its 'unnational' nature.

By the beginning of the occupation, Danish musicians had learned how to play. The Afro-American competition, their teachers and model, was back home. Respectable people joined Hot Clubs modelled after Delaunay's in cities and university centres all over the country. Jazz music miraculously became less 'bestial' when played by Danes.

The white/black, European/American controversy is still part of daily conversation among French musicians. It is confused conversation, and in the social context of the music with the political situation of the time, the following editorial in the September 1943 edition of *Jazz Hot* titled 'The White and the Black', carries confusion to hallucinating proportions:

> If in America prejudice exists, even when it comes to music, against the blacks, the contrary prejudice seems to exist in France. Americans do not seem to be aware that jazz owes everything to the blacks; here the situation is the reverse. This is ridiculous. The public falls in love with the first Negro who comes over and who can bang on the top of a box, while only admitting the value and talent of white musicians with great reluctance. Certain members of the Hot Club withhold applause for players like Hubert Rostaing, who can compete very well with blacks. Our musicians have made great progress. . .

That same year, Asmussen reopened the great Danish jazz debate by taking a public Crow Jim stand: 'Jazz is stagnating in this country because white people will never be able to master a music which blacks have in their blood when they are born.'

So in his book *Jazz in Denmark*, Erik Wiedemann covers more than just Denmark when he concludes:

> The reception of jazz in Denmark during [World War II] was to a large extent influenced by five myths: 1) the racist one that jazz

is a music created by sub-human beings, 2) the chauvinist one that jazz is a primitive and exotic music and a threat to European culture, 3) the racist one (with a difference) that jazz is only for blacks because they are born with it, 4) the biological one that jazz is a 'natural' music because all children are born with it, and 5) the aesthetic one that jazz is folk, not art, music . . . These myths, which were often combined . . . were all contradicted by the evolution of the music itself. . .

One morning at five, a Danish-speaking Gestapo officer wearing a black hat and black trenchcoat knocked on Asmussen's door and said, 'Come with me.' The same night they arrested 500 prominent Danes – politicians, scientists, writers, show-business people – as hostages against a threatened general strike. For a month he sat in a makeshift camp in Copenhagen. When they took him to the Alexanderplatz prison in Berlin there was still no formal charge against him. He spent seven weeks there. He was not allowed to lie on the cot during the day. He could never tell if anyone was looking through the peep-hole in the door, but if they did they surely thought he was crazy because to keep from going crazy he jitterbugged and sang 'Alexander's Ragtime Band' like mad for hours.

His family got in touch with Herr Hermansen, a Gestapo officer in Copenhagen who Asmussen describes as a 'secret anti-Nazi'. He was from the north-west part of Germany that used to belong to Denmark: 'This man of honour did not Heil Hitler. He must have got several hundred Danes released from German prisons. He managed to transfer my case to another officer like himself. Herr Hermansen never got any recognition for any of it; after the war he was sent to prison for being a Nazi.'

Banned from the radio in 1940, jazz reappeared in 1943 for thirty minutes a day at exactly the same time as the BBC Danish-language broadcast. Its popularity can be measured by the fact that the Germans considered it the strongest programming for such tough competition.

It can get dark early and cold quickly in Provence in the winter. We get up and I pack up and Svend Asmussen will drive me to the train. Something about the sudden change reminds me of a poem by Jim Morrison, a line of which I almost picked as the title.

> Enter again the sweet forest.
> Enter the hot dream.
> Come with us.
> Everything is broken up and dances.

How could it all be so broken up and still dance? So sweet and so hot at the same time? It is difficult to connect the heat of the dream, more a nightmare, to a sweet forest; a forest in the Ardennes where you find an old shoe with a foot in it.

'Svend. People have told me . . . Is it true? Would you call World War II the "Golden Age of Jazz"?'

'Yes, it is so. At that time jazz music had the same broad appeal as rock today, even broader. Every generation listened to it. With young people it was a provocation, particularly against the Germans, who were really irritated by this American music. It was symbolic, true, but it was also very popular dance music. Older people loved to dance to jazz. People with money, important people, cultured people, invited us to play for dancing at their parties. Jazz, always jazz, jazz is what they wanted.'

20
The Angels Sing

Jazz, jazz, all they wanted was jazz.

Eight young coalminers from eastern France formed a jazz band, rehearsed evenings and weekends and paid their own way to play in Paris. More enthusiastic than accomplished, they were not acclaimed by the Parisian press. Provincials and defenders of the working class accused critics of being 'Centralist Zazou Plutocrats'.

Popular accordion-propelled events tried fusing swing with tango. In *La Vie Parisienne sous l'Occupation*, Hervé le Boterf writes about a 'From Tango to Swing' concert, in Salle Pleyel in 1944:

> The audience was rather reserved during the first half of the concert consecrated to the tango. When the curtain rose for the second, swing, half, there were cheers, 'bravo, bravo'. The tango singer Ricardo Bravo thought that he was being called back for an encore, but when he returned to the stage he was hissed and booed. Tango had no choice but to recognize the supremacy of swing.

There were 185 professional drummers registered in Paris in 1943.

The rich and the privileged threw all-night curfew parties. It was a wonderful feeling, an airtight excuse, to be forced to party until dawn. Nobody could accuse you of decadence or dissipation; you were just obeying the law. And they wanted jazz, the music the enemy hated. Swing was a political statement. A party with a swing band was a form of resistance, without one you were just fiddling while Rome burned.

One morning, in the Neuilly *pavillon* of the Dominican Republic's playboy ambassador Porfirio Rubirosa, married to actress Danielle Darrieux, Rubirosa paid the band overtime to continue for himself alone after the guests had gone. He had a small day today. Django Reinhardt had refused to play all night. Rare – he generally came with and brought down the house. Pierre Fouad claimed Django owed him some money, and the king couldn't be bothered with such small change. He sulked and complained to Rubirosa, royalty to royalty, about Fouad's presence. As the morning wore on, however, he picked up his Maccaferri and after jamming all afternoon Django said to Fouad: 'People who can play music together should be friends.'

This morning, a letter arrived from Vienna. I've been expecting it. It's late. It probably belongs further up somewhere but this is the final draft and anyway most of it contains previously processed information, with new names and dates. How many times can you read, 'Jazz saved my life', or 'This was the Golden Age of jazz?' A few stories, however, do contribute to our degree of insanity.

Herbert Mitteis practised acting crazy with the help of great quantities of schnapps. He was a good actor; his act got him discharged from the German army. A doctor declared him clinically insane. He collected umbrellas, eyeglasses and items like that, or stole them, and the next day he sold these things between sets in the Viennese cafes where he played jazz. Some people thought he was really crazy. Artur Motta, nicknamed Tutur, was under forced labour in Germany until being returned home to Vienna in 1943, after which he played in a band with Ernst Landl and Herbert Mitteis in a hotel bar in the Centrum. The German officers who came to dance often asked them to 'play it hot'. They requested 'Cootie Cootie' and 'Joseph Joseph', an Andrews Sisters hit based on a Yiddish song which was forbidden because, in addition, Joseph was Goebbels' first name. The title had been changed to 'She Does Not Want Flowers and Chocolate'; and 'St Louis Blues' was called 'Sauerkraut' in Vienna. Vienna Reichsrundfunk was the principal antenna for Nazi propaganda to eastern Europe. The authorities decided they needed a lively big band, like Charly in Berlin, that would project a swinging Viennese ambience. They did not credit 'Summertime' as having been written by George Gershwin. Contemporary Viennese collectors still have some of their transcriptions, mild and derivative swing music mixed with propaganda. There were musicians from France, Greece and Bulgaria in this band, and a trombone player – nobody was sure of his nationality at the time and the letter-writer does not remember his name. Presumably from Latvia, he had four passports and some say he was Jewish. When the Royal Air Force bombed Vienna, he would stick his trombone out the window and play 'Sauerkraut' instead of hiding in the cellar. He was just as crazy as Herbert Mitteis.

While working on this book, all sorts of crazy 'symbolic deeds of sinister significance' kept happening to me and to those around me. It was as though some Aryan sorcerer was sticking pins in *entartete* dolls. I lost twelve kilos; a film-maker producing a documentary about surviving SS officers working about the same time as myself lost about the same amount of weight and had similar experiences. The Third Reich refuses to stay in the past. It's a spell, a curse, something hanging in the air which provokes evil deeds with its 'strange complacent consciousness'.

Claude Verses believed that the German nationality of the woman behind his misfortune was of sinister significance, and that it was directly related to my book. But he began to get some breaks after his release from prison, which I pointed out to him. He said: 'No. Brakes.'

He sold his essay on Klaus Barbie to the *Atlantic Monthly*. I read that one, but the rest is only his word. *Playboy* bought a piece tying together decadence and gangsters in Berlin and Las Vegas. He said he sold eight poems to the *New Yorker*, a screenplay to Stephen Spielberg and signed two big contracts involving large advances for novels with Doubleday.

He dressed in designer clothes, ordered red Sancerre in Brasserie Lipp and the owner knew his name, he left his Citroën CX with the doorman of the expensive remodelled seventeenth-century hotel where he lived, wrote in the Cafe Flore in the afternoon. But Albert Camus once wrote that every man over forty is 'responsible for his own face'. The face of Claude Verses was becoming something you would not claim responsibility for. When France asked why he spent so much time in the toilet, he said he was taking medicine for a large intestinal problem. It was not clear what was large, the intestine or the problem.

He claimed to be only waiting for the police to return his passport – they had held it for a year already – before flying ('First-class, you get there first') to Paraguay: 'First-class folks down there. First-class all the way. I'm going to retire and hire five nubile sisters to fan my ass all day long.'

The weather in Paraguay is not particularly hot and being fanned by nubile sisters isn't considered cool by the sisters themselves, but he was not living in what is sometimes referred to as 'the real world'.

His mail was forwarded to our address. There were frequent large (but not large enough to attract attention) dollar cheques from publishing houses I had never heard of. When he came to pick them up, he would stay for 'a nightcap' often lasting several nights. He bore gifts, like a bicycle for Robbie. The two of them played Monopoly for hours. Verses called our house 'Get out of Jail Free House'.

Postcards from Blow Black with photos of Bangkok, Amsterdam, La Paz and Ascunsion on them were written in German. (Blow was retired with pension from the studios.) When he flew in from Lausanne, where he now lives, once a month or so, Verses picked him up in his CX and the two of them registered in the Plaza Athenée Hotel. 'Blow,' explained Verses, 'is trading futures.'

Once he brought me a magnum of Chivas Regal, and I asked if he had robbed a bank. 'I don't have to rob a bank,' he said. 'I own a bank.'

'You own a bank?' Robbie rubbed his hands. 'Do you want to buy Park Lane?'

'Sure. Five million Paraguayan pesetas.'

'How much is that?'

'Thirty francs.'

'Sold.' Robbie ran off to get the title and when he came back he asked where Paraguay was. I showed him in an atlas.

'What do the people do there?' he asked.

'They make fertilizer.' Verses thought that was very funny.

I told him to cut that shit out. Not much slips by this kid. France wanted to cut Verses out period and I was beginning to agree with her. Mumblers with German accents were telephoning at odd hours. Hearing unusual sounds in the entrance, France drew a deep breath: 'It's the police.'

But Verses did not have many friends; I do not have many myself, and participating in family life was obviously precious to him. We talked writers' talk; he was the only person I could do that with. He's a black casualty of white society. I felt a sense of responsibility.

Then one night I was awakened from a deep sleep. It was neither the elevator nor the square-wheeled tricycles. Somebody was sobbing. I looked at the clock – 5.22. Probably a drunken neighbour. I tried to find my sleep again but the sounds grew longer and louder, the silence between them grew shorter and they were coming from our living-room.

The lamp was lit; Verses was sitting on the couch in his underwear with open sightless eyes. He went: 'AAAAGGGHHHH....' I get the shivers just writing it. It has been in my head ever since. Terror, the sound of terror. The externalization of the roar of my own loneliness. The devil's roar. I touched his shoulder: 'Verses?'

'TWINS!!!' he screamed. 'TWINS!!!'

I shook him: 'What's wrong, Claude?'

'TWINS!!! WHERE ARE ALL THE TWINS? WHOSE TWIN AM I?' Then, louder – much louder: 'AAAAAGGGGHHHHHH!!!!!' He was sweating, twitching, scratching. I shook him very hard: 'VERSES!'

He turned his head, his eyes suddenly wide-open, and asked in a normal tone of voice: 'What time is it?'

I told him.

'Must have been dreaming,' he groaned. 'Was I saying anything?'

'Something about twins.'

He jumped. I thought he might lose control again. I fetched a wet towel, placed it on his forehead and poured a tumbler of Chivas. He gulped it down. Shaking, he went to take a shower.

Yesterday's *Herald Tribune* was on the floor near the couch. 'OUCH WITS!' was hand-written next to a front-page headline: 'Mengele was Involved in Drug Trafficking, CIA Reports Hint'. The article read:

The Central Intelligence Agency began receiving reports in 1971 that Dr Josef Mengele, the Nazi war criminal, was heavily involved with partners in illegal narcotics trafficking in Paraguay ... Dr Mengele was the chief doctor at the Auschwitz death camp, where millions of people died ...The CIA also suggested that the business owned by Dr Mengele's family, a German farm machinery manufacturing company with offices in South America, 'could serve as a mechanism to move or launder large sums of money, as well as to cover the movement of illicit narcotics'.

He came out of the bathroom, glanced at the article and at me, dressed quickly and went for the door. Verses raised his eyes and looked into mine and we kissed on both cheeks. 'Unblest historicity,' he said. 'Finish your book.'

Django Reinhardt was offered 80,000 francs per concert to tour Germany. Though he was in debt he said less than 120,000 would damage his professional standing. There had been previous offers at lower prices and this escalation could not go on for ever. Even though his fame protected himself and his family, he knew what was happening to Gypsies in Germany.

As Paris began to receive its share of bombs, Django spent more and more time in the Pigalle metro station. Sometimes he'd dive down there before a siren even sounded. It was time to get out of town.

He went to Thonon-Les-Bains, near the Swiss border on Lake Léman. It seemed like as good a place as any. There were plenty of Gypsies in the hills and they came down visit him. Half of them seemed to be guitar players.

They jammed every night in a restaurant, a *Gajo* rhythm section arrived from Paris. The public grew, people rode bicycles from neighbouring villages in the dark. Django the Gypsy king was in town. There were poker games, billiard matches and feasts. Here's this well-known face on his way across a tightly policed border from a country at war and he makes it a party. 'Hey folks, just sneaking through.'

It was impossible to live in Thonon without being infected by the nearby border and the lights of neutral Switzerland on the other side of the lake. Being that close to 'free people' made these particular occupied people somehow freer. Ordinary Frenchmen, German soldiers and spies sat side by side to listen to the guitar with the human voice.

France's uncle Yves was a teenager in the resistance around

there and he remembers listening to Django while sitting next to a table of SS officers. Everybody knew the war was almost over; the Germans were collecting clemency credits like the officers who picked up Eric Vogel, at just about the same time, come to think of it. Yves was guiding two RAF officers who had parachuted over the Jura to Switzerland. One of them exclaimed: 'I say old chap, jolly good guitarman there.'

Two Germans looked at each other as though wondering if they shouldn't put these chaps on the rack just to keep their reputation. Finally, one of them said (in English too): 'He's right, you know.'

Yves was a radio operator up in the mountains with a unit that had the responsibility to light bonfires to guide the RAF over the Alps on their way to bomb Italy. London broadcast a signal in code five minutes before the bombers were to pass over their sector. The code was Martha Tilton singing 'And the Angels Sing' with the Benny Goodman band.

Yves remembers Django playing the 'Marseillaise' one night in Thonon.

'What did the Germans do? Sing the "Horst Wessel Song" like in *Casablanca*?'

'No. It was much too late for that. The "Horst Wessel Song" was out of style. Even the Germans, no, particularly the Germans, didn't want to hear the "Horst Wessel Song". But you know ...' Yves hesitated as though not believing his own memory: 'Everybody, but everybody in town knew that he was going to make a break for it. He discussed it openly with his cousins – every Gypsy within fifty kilometres of Thonon seemed to be his cousin. They'd sit around the table drinking cognac discussing what route to take.'

Of course he was caught. The police found his English Society of Composers membership card. This by itself could have been enough to hang him as a spy. But the German officer began his interrogation with a smile: '*Mon vieux Reinhardt, que fais-tu là!*' (Django my man, what are you doing here?) and freed him with a warning. Another jazz fan, another life saved by jazz.

His inaccessibility had made Django something of a legend in the US, where the press had reported several rumours of his death. After the liberation he played at an army party in Paris. Considering America the big time, wanting to tour there badly, having dreamed about it for so long, he played particularly hard. He was, however, quite cool answering an official who asked how much he would want for an American tour.

'How much does Gary Cooper make?' he asked. 'I want the same thing.'

He had learned something about the value of swing.

But he had been a big fish in a small, artificially dammed, remote pond. When, after the war, he heard that phonograph record with the red label, Charlie Parker and Dizzy Gillespie playing 'Salt Peanuts', he shook his head and said: 'How do they play that fast? I don't know if I can keep up with them.' To mix a metaphor, he had been king of what turned out to be a small hill, and it began to collapse under him. His kingdom was a fairy-tale land.

In 1946, he received a cable from New York that read: 'You must come right away. Wonderful contract for you. Let me know when you will arrive. Duke Ellington.' It looked as though his Manhattan dream was coming true. He did not reply to the cable because he did not have enough money to buy a transatlantic ticket, or a credit rating enabling him to borrow it. He did not know what to say; better say nothing.

He left two weeks later. The tour had been postponed. He left without a guitar, no luggage, not even a toothbrush. He was expecting a ticker-tape parade worthy of a head of state, he would certainly be showered with gifts. Showrooms and vaults would be at his disposal. It did not turn out that way.

He borrowed the money to buy a guitar and the concerts in Cleveland, Chicago, Detroit, Kansas City and Pittsburgh went well. The sign in front of Carnegie Hall read: 'The Duke Ellington orchestra, with special guest Django Reinhardt, the most acclaimed guitarist in the world.'

There are many versions of what actually happened that night, but everyone agrees about one thing. He was late. Ellington's orchestra had begun the third number. Ellington was nervous. After pacing in the wings, he took the microphone and, his voice cracking with emotion, announced: 'For reasons beyond our control, the famous guitarist Django Reinhardt will not be appearing tonight on this stage. I am just as disappointed as you are. Maybe he will arrive before the end of the concert. Maybe you will still be able to hear him. Please excuse us, I beg you. I love you madly.'

One version has Django being finally found facing a long line of empty beer bottles. Another involves a taxi-driver who took him to Queens. Still another has him losing track of time watching his friend and fellow Frenchman Marcel Cerdan win a boxing match, which took longer than expected. When he finally arrived, he had no guitar. One was found but there was no time to tune it. The New York critics were not kind.

He blamed everything and everybody but himself. American guitars were 'tinny'. He told Charles Delaunay that he did not like the American mentality. American women were all 'frigid' and the only way he could score was by renting nude models to come to his hotel room to be 'sketched'. He did not even like American cars; seeing so many of his beloved limousines together somehow diminished his own royalty.

He had an engagement in Cafe Society, on 52nd Street, and the crowds were large but the management called him 'unprofessional and unco-operative' because he refused to play encores. He said he was only trying to fulfil his contract, which of course he couldn't read.

He spent evenings with Cerdan and the French singer Jean Sablon, who says that they often wandered around Broadway until dawn. Django was amazed with himself, he missed France so much: the food, the cigarettes, he had not thought he was so French.

Returning to Paris, he played in the caves of St Germain, tried to master the electric guitar and bebop – and then he died in Samois.

24 November 1946, the night when Django Reinhardt kept Duke Ellington waiting on the stage of Carnegie Hall, marked his own abdication, and the end of the 'Golden Age of Jazz' he had presided over.

Citing any one specific date or event as a benchmark is bound to be somewhat arbitrary, but Django no longer had the leverage to be tardy and jazz would never again be art for the masses.

It would influence mass art, it would be a prime influence, it would certainly become more artistic. But it only reached a broad spectrum of age, class and race when fused, usually watered-down, with more commercial music. It can be argued that jazz continued to have political clout in Eastern Europe for similar reasons as in Nazi Germany, but in fact it reached only the young and dissident. There was never *mass* support.

The 'Golden Age of Jazz' coincided with the rise of the Third Reich, was limited to the territory it occupied and ended with the liberation, and that is certainly no coincidence.

We are left with nostalgia – with Hans Bluthner, Otto Jung and Charles Delaunay with their old records, closing doors to keep out the new, reminiscing, researching personnel in reference books, gathering dust. Like Delaunay, jazz is no longer 'in the game'.

The gold had been tarnished all along, symbol more than music. 'I love the music my enemy hates.' If Goebbels had swung to 'St Louis Blues' instead of banning it, there would have been no 'Tristesse de Saint Louis', no 'Golden Age'.

And so it came to pass that a devil named Joseph Goebbels was the most powerful angel jazz music ever had, but the gold turned to dust when the devil died and the love died with the hate.

Sources

Batashev, Alexei *The Soviet Jazz* (Izdatelstvo 'Muzika')

Beauvoir, Simone de *The Prime of Life* (Colophon Books, Harper)

Cobb, Richard *French and Germans, Germans and French* (Brandeis, New England)

Collins & Lapierre *Is Paris Burning?* (Pocket)

Coeuroy, André *Histoire Générale de Jazz* (Denoel)

Deighton, Len *Fighter* (Panther)

Delaunay, Charles *Django Reinhardt* (Da Capo)

Dutourd, Jean *Au Bon Beurre* (Folio)

Goebbels, Joseph *Final Diaries, 1945* (Avon)

Heiber, Helmut *Goebbels, a Biography* (Da Capo)

Higham, Charles *Trading with the Enemy* (Dell)

Le Boterf, Hervé *La Vie Parisienne sous l'Occupation* (France-Empire)

Loiseau, Jean-Claude *Les Zazous* (Sagittaire)

Ophuls, Marcel *The Sorrow and the Pity* (Outerbridge and Lazard)

Panassié, Hugues *Monsieur Jazz* (Stock)

Paxton, Robert O. *Vichy France* (Norton Library)

Salgues, Yves 'La Légende de Django Reinhardt' (*Jazz* magazine)

Schoenbrun, David *Soldiers of the Night* (Meridian)

Shirer, William L. *The Rise and Fall of the Third Reich* (Pan)

Skvorecky, Joseph *The Bass Saxophone* (Picador)

— 'Hipness at Noon' (*New Republic* magazine)

Vémane, Henri *Swing et Moeurs* (Editions des Marchenelles)

Vercours *Le Silence de la Mer* (Albin Michel)

Wiedmann, Erik *Jazz in Denmark* (Gyldenal)

Wiener, Jean *Allegro Appassionato* (Belfond)

Index